Minef … M…crophones

Global Asymmetric Warfare, the Radical Left, and Winning the War on Terror

To Mike—
Semper Fi!

"Gunny" Bob Newman USMC (Ret.)

GunnyBob

Minefields to Microphones:
Global Asymmetric Warfare, the Radical Left,
and Winning the War on Terror
by "Gunny" Bob Newman USMC (Ret.)

ISBN 10: 1-58160-557-9
ISBN 13: 978-1-58160-557-0
Printed in the United States of America

Published by Paladin Press, a division of
Paladin Enterprises, Inc.
Gunbarrel Tech Center
7077 Winchester Circle
Boulder, Colorado 80301 USA
+1.303.443.7250

Direct inquiries and/or orders to the above address.

Visit the author's Web site at www.850koa.com/pages/shows_gunny.html

Visit our Web site at www.paladin-press.com

Table of Contents

To my friend, confidant, brother, and former commanding officer, Colonel Bryan P. "Darkside" McCoy USMC.

Those harp seals had it coming, Bryan.

Acknowledgments

I owe many people a great deal.

If any of you are waiting for me to pay you back, you will be waiting quite a while, as I have no means to do so. You did that much for me.

The following should consider themselves acknowledged.

In the Corps and Navy:

Colonel Bryan P. "Darkside" McCoy USMC; Lieutenant Colonel J.W. Muth III USMC (retired); Lieutenant Colonel (formerly Staff Sergeant) Todd P. Ohman USMC; Sergeant Patrick Halling USMC; Sergeant William "Mandingo, the Ebony Prince" Jones USMC; Gunnery Sergeant J.D. Bishop USMC (retired); Sergeant Major C.T. Garr USMC (retired); Staff Sergeant John Moch USMC; Lieutenant Colonel John Bass USMC (retired); 1st Sergeant Brad Delauter USMC (retired); Major Keith Kelly USMC (retired); Lieutenant Colonel Douglas Rapé USMC (retired); Colonel Kevin A. Conry USMC (retired); Sergeant Major M.D. "Mad Dog" Turner USMC (retired); Colonel J.J. Carty USMC (retired); Commander Bob Fant, U.S. Navy (retired); Master Chief Petty Officer Tom Keith, U.S. Navy SEALs (retired); Gunnery Sergeant David V. Bowen USMC (retired); Sergeant Major George Misko USMC (retired); Petty Officer William

"Doc" Morgan, U.S. Navy; 1st Lieutenant Timothy A. Sloan USMC; 1st Sergeant Rick Pelow USMC (retired); and Lieutenant Colonel Gary Colpas USMC (retired)

At Clear Channel:

Robin Bertolucci, Don Martin, Mark Remington, Kris Olinger, Jerry Bell, Amani Ali, Mike O'Connor, Pat Connor, Lee Larsen, Mike Rosen, Dave Logan, Scott Hastings (now with Altitude Sports), Alex Stone (now with ABC), Dominic Bond, Peter Boyles, Steve Kelley (now with Fox 31), April Zesbaugh, and Tyler Moody (now with CNN)

At Paladin Press:

Peder Lund and Jon Ford

At Blackhawk Products Group:

Michael Janich

At FOX News Channel:

Bill O'Reilly, Laurie Dhue, John Gibson, Greta van Susteren, Shepard Smith, Major General Paul Vallely, U.S. Army (retired), and Colonel David Hunt, U.S. Army (retired)

At MSNBC:

Rita Cosby, Monica Crowley, Ron Reagan, Susan Durrwachter, and Tony Maciulis

At *Westword*:

Michael Roberts

In politics:

Gov. Bill Owens, Sen. Wayne Allard, Rep. Tom Tancredo, and Rep. Bob Beauprez

Elsewhere in the media:
Michelle Malkin, Gloria Neal, Harvey Kushner, Ph.D., the late Johnnie Cochran, David Petzal, Elizabeth Estes-Cooper, David Horowitz, and Scott Redmond

At The GeoScope Group:
Larry Huwa

At All Pro Sports & Entertainment:
Peter Schaffer

In Derangedville:
Michael Floorwax, Rick Lewis, Kathy Lee and the "G Man"

In Maine:
Bill Newman

Minding the camp and campus, respectively:
My wife, Susan, and daughter, Britta

In Memoriam

Mary Jane (McDonald) Newman
3 August 1928–25 January 1993

Rocky the Yellow Labrador
1 January 1992–22 April 2005

Ruger the Cat
12 October 1990–6 August 2004

"My idea of a fair fight is clubbing baby harp seals."

Lieutenant Colonel Bryan P. "Darkside" McCoy USMC, Commanding Officer, 3rd Battalion, 4th Marines, addressing his Marines before they attacked into Iraq, 16 March 2003

Introduction

We knew something was up.

It was the spring of 1980 and I was a sergeant in a Marine reconnaissance platoon in the North Arabian Sea aboard the USS *Okinawa* (LPH 3 or landing pad, helicopter), an antediluvian warship carrying part of the 31st Marine Amphibious Unit out of the Marine base at Kaneohe Bay, Hawaii. I'd been in the Corps three years and had been a sergeant for a little over one.

In my platoon's berth, the platoon's noncommissioned officers, or NCOs, were discussing the situation, which was one none of us had exactly been in before.

Just outside the Straits of Hormuz, which separate the North Arabian Sea from the Persian Gulf, the Marines of 3rd Platoon, Alpha Company, 3rd Reconnaissance Battalion considered the facts.

We were very close to the coast to Iran and could, in fact, see the red dust of Asia on the horizon. Muslim terrorists who had removed Mohammed Reza Pahlavi, the Shah of Iran, from the Peacock Throne had taken dozens of Americans hostage when the United States Embassy in Tehran was sacked and were threatening to kill them. As members of the Marine Corps' only type of unit that was specifically trained in special operations, we all knew that we could quickly find ourselves doing something extraordinarily dangerous in the middle of a maritime nowhere.

How nowhere? Our patrol area was nicknamed Gonzo Station.

A day after we had left Pearl Harbor, a Soviet spy "trawler" had picked up our four-ship group. The small ship, which was an intelligence-collection vessel, had stuck with us for months. Now it was a problem and a potentially big problem at that.

If a rescue mission were to be launched from the *Okinawa* or *Nimitz* to extract the hostages from the hands of their captors, that little trawler could detect the mission and inform Moscow, which could then warn Tehran, thus completely eliminating the offensive principle of surprise.

My reconnaissance team aboard the USS *Okinawa*, April 1980. Note the rapelling gear and personal flotation devices, as we were conducting rapelling training off the side of the ship. From left to right: the author, Jim Ingalls, Charlie Cordova, Stan "The Man" Iramk, and Bill Fanning.

This meant my platoon might have to board the Soviet vessel, kill the crew, and scuttle the ship.

Heavily armed American Marines committing an overt act of war on the Soviet Union by boarding a Soviet ship and sending her to the bottom of the sea after shooting the crew. Now there's a scenario that will make you sit up and pay attention, given that a Marine reconnaissance platoon's actions in the unlikely North Arabian Sea might lead to global thermonuclear warfare (we figured the Soviets would not take kindly to our attack).

One plan was to use a helicopter to get onto the vessel by rappelling from the chopper onto the trawler. Another plan was to avoid the use of a chopper to gain a purchase on the deck of the trawler for fear the Soviets would shoot the bird down with us still in it. Instead, under cover of a moonless night, we would "helo cast" (jump from the chopper from a height of about 20 feet into the sea at a speed of about 20 knots) into the path of the trawler and when it came by us, with the crew not knowing we were in the water beside them, toss grappling hooks onto the deck and pull ourselves aboard, quickly kill the crew, and sink her. Before our chopper took off, we would have the *Nimitz* launch an EA-6B Prowler electronic-warfare jet to jam the trawler's communications and eavesdropping ability. We'd still have to board the trawler and kill the crew just in case the jamming failed.

A more cockamamie scheme had seldom been hatched by Marines. But as crazy as our plan was, we were convinced we could pull it off. We were that good—and that cocky.

As it were, our mission was never ordered for whatever reason and the hostage rescue mission named "Eagle Claw" conducted by Delta Force terminated in a massive ball of fire at Desert One. The mission commander, Army Colonel "Chargin' Charlie" Beckwith, immediately blamed everything and everyone but himself for the disaster.

America's first foray into the world of counterterrorism was a miserable failure.

As we sailed from the North Arabian Sea to Mombasa, Kenya, we considered what our former company commander, Captain Jack Muth III USMC, a former enlisted reconnaissance man in Vietnam, had told us as he began turning the company from a strictly reconnaissance unit into a special operations unit in the late 1970s. He said that some day the Corps' primary mission would likely be hunting and killing terrorists. To that end, some members of the company were trained at the FBI Academy in Quantico in hostage-rescue techniques and other "sexy" missions.

Three years later, I would find myself stationed in West Germany at the height of terrorism there. Such terrorist groups as the Red Army Faction (formerly the Baader-Meinhof Gang), Communist Combatant Cells, Black September, Action Direct, Red Brigades, al Fatah, Japanese Red Army, Irish Republican Army, and ETA were very active and very dangerous in Europe, killing many people. Detailed searches of vehicles entering military bases were routine, and we always checked our vehicles before we got in them in case a bomb was under the hood, under the car, or atop a tire hidden by the wheel well.

One October evening in late 1983, I received a phone call in my apartment in Frankfurt from Captain Doug Rapé USMC, who was assigned to the U.S. Consulate there. He instructed me to report to him first thing in the morning for a temporary duty assignment expected to last a few weeks. I was about to become the Marine Corps' liaison to the FBI forensics team coming to Frankfurt to identify the bodies of 241 Marines and sailors (and a handful of soldiers) who had just been killed by a Hezbollah truck bomb in Beirut. The words of Captain Muth came back to me: *some day the Corps' primary mission would likely be hunting and killing terrorists.*

Four years later, I was selected by Headquarters, U.S. Marine Corps (HQMC), as one of a team of four Marines to become the Naval Service's first formally trained and certified survival-evasion-resistance-escape (SERE) instructors. After passing the SERE course and the SERE instructor-training program, I was asked by Commander Bob Fant, U.S. Navy (retired), a former prisoner of war who ran the advanced SERE course, to become the Corps' first certified advanced SERE instructor. That billet required me to teach hostage survival and terrorism avoidance techniques to deploying sailors and Marines who had already graduated from the basic SERE course. Among other training, I was sent to the U.S. Air Force's Special Operations School at Hurlburt Field, Florida, to attend the Dynamics of International Terrorism (DIT) Course, which is jointly taught by the U.S. Air Force, CIA, FBI, and other people.

The author as a SERE instructor north of "The Horn" aboard the Redington Training Facility, summer 1988.

As a student at DIT, my eyes were thrown open upon learning just how big, as in global, the war against terrorists was going to become. And I wondered how it was that my path kept bringing me back to the world of terrorism.

While at DIT in the late 1980s, some fellow students and I discussed ways terrorists could attack inside America. One of the means we came up with was pilot-trained terrorists hijacking or stealing commercial jetliners and crashing them into high-value targets, such as nuclear reactor domes, the White House, Congress, and chemical plants. It seemed far-fetched at first, but after we studied the details of what training, logistics, intelligence, and security would be required for such an attack, we realized it was quite doable.

In early 1990, having begun writing professionally on the side, I queried the editor of the *Marine Corps Gazette* and proposed I write an article on terrorism and how it related to the Marine Corps' future combat operations. Colonel John Greenwood USMC (retired), wrote back and said the *Gazette* was not interested in such an article because the Corps would seldom if ever be involved with terrorists despite what had occurred in Beirut. I wondered how someone as

A Marine comedian placed this sticker on a destroyed Iraqi tank that had been hit in the turret with an armor-piercing round. Author's photo.

I found this photo of Saddam in an Iraqi munitions bunker in al Jahra.

naive and uninformed as Colonel Greenwood could have made it to his terminal rank.

In late February 1991, standing with my infantry company on the 6th Ring Road in al Jahra (a western suburb of Kuwait City), I was stunned to hear over the radio that Saddam had thrown in the towel and would be allowed to stay in power.

I knew then the Marines would be back to finish the job, years later. And I had a bad feeling that I would again find my path crossing into the realm of terrorists, but I had no idea when, where, or in what capacity.

On 9-11, I was shaving in my home in Colorado when my wife shouted for me to come downstairs and look at the television, which was showing a gaping hole with smoke pouring out of one of the World Trade Center towers. The first thing I noticed was that the sky over Manhattan that morning was a bright blue. This was no accident caused by bad weather. I recalled our discussions at DIT.

Then the second plane hit and I cursed. "They did it. They pulled it off just like we figured they could," I said aloud. Then, "They're going to pay for this shit." Within minutes I was calling old friends from the Corps, all special operations and reconnaissance types, and we plotted our return to the Corps from retirement. Surely the Corps would want seasoned "SpecOps" killers like us to return to the fold for immediate deployment to wherever the war would be. Of course, we are all partially disabled and the Corps politely refused our reenlistment requests.

Thanks, Gunny, but we can handle it.

A month later, I was hired by Clear Channel, Inc., as a military science and terrorism analyst, a job that quickly expanded into talk-show host.

Clear Channel brought me aboard after I sent them an e-mail telling them that some of the self-proclaimed military and terrorism experts who had come out of the woodwork to become green-room commandos on cable television did not have the qualifications they claimed to have and were passing bum scoop. I attached my curricula vitae to the e-mail, they investigated and interviewed me, tested me on the air, and hired me.

Driving home after being hired, in my mind I had to thank a vice president at the Lexington Institute, a beltway think tank. His analysis one day in October 2001 was what finally caused me to send that e-mail to Clear Channel. This man, a "military analyst" for MSNBC, had told a host that the U.S. Army's 10th Mountain Division would likely attack into Afghanistan from Uzbekistan via parachute drop. Of course, the man's assessment was ludicrous, and I knew right then that he was one of many media people pretending to be a military strategist, when in reality he had spent, at least according to his bio, nary a day in the armed forces; his entire career had been spent in academia and the theoretical world of military make-believe.

By November 2001, FOX News Channel was calling frequently. Soon I was talking on a regular basis to the likes of Rita Cosby, Bill O'Reilly, John Gibson, Geraldo Rivera, Laurie Dhue, Greta van Susteren, Shepard Smith et al about the war on terror. Then it was MSNBC, CBS, NBC, ABC, WB, the BBC, *Newsweek*, the *Chicago Tribune*, Reuters, CNN, Agence France-Presse, Australian radio and television, and so on. Security conferences began to call and ask for presentations; I was off to London, Hong Kong, Dubai, Shanghai, Singapore, Washington D.C., and New York City, in the latter of which I picked up a National Edward R. Murrow Award for investigative reporting on homeland security and the war on terror. Senators and congressmen began calling, wanting to be on my shows. Two newspaper columns came along, as did a handful of Internet news website columns.

Yes, all this was unexpected and at times quite dizzying to a retired Marine grunt from the coast of Maine and Florida's Everglades. Hell, I didn't even expect to survive the Corps. And as all this unfolded, I made sure to continually remind myself that this was happening because of what the Marine Corps had given me and not because I was something special or unique or because I was so brilliant.

By October 2005, I had managed to amass the best record in the media for a military science and terrorism analyst when it came to publicly made, accurate, specific predictions and assessments in the war on terror, and stories broken (113 in five years as of this writing). I had even briefed a Congressional caucus on homeland security and the war on terror as they pertain to immigration, and in the first week of October 2005, the president of the United States confirmed my numerous reports of the last four years that told of al Qaeda reconnaissance teams inside the United States conducting target reconnaissance and that some of those teams were being monitored by the FBI. I had been taking a lot of heat because of those reports, with some people who don't like me claiming I was making it all up and chastising me for not revealing how I knew about these operational terrorist recon cells in America. When the president said in a speech before the National Endowment for Democracy that we had indeed been monitoring al Qaeda recon teams and that at least three major attacks inside the U.S. had been prevented because the FBI had been conducting surveillance on the teams, I was not only vindicated but relieved to a degree.

How could a Marine gunnery sergeant pull off such stunts?

I am in the media, that's how. I'm no modern-day Nostradamus. The fact of the matter is that there are other Marines who could have done the same thing I've done so far—if they had a microphone and if they had a television camera to look in to. There are some Marines who could have done it better, I suspect.

Scratch "suspect." *Know.*

In the end, it comes down to training, experience, curiosity, initiative, and, perhaps most importantly, a willingness and ability to develop intelligence assets I could use in my various jobs within the media. Like I said, I am far from the only Marine who could do this. I just happened to be the one who did it. And if Marine Corps initiative hadn't insisted I send that e-mail to Clear Channel, I probably never would have done it.

This book is a result not only of my record as a very successful military science and terrorism analyst but because so many people who listen to my radio show, watch me on television, and read my columns, wanted the book.

Herein you will read how and why I think the way I do, how I've been able to become so good as a war-on-terror analyst and controversial-to-some political pundit (a danger of the job that comes with the territory called "radio talk-show host"), and what we can expect in the many years to come as the war on terror spreads far and wide.

You'll pardon me if I sugarcoat nothing. If you want kinder and gentler, or if you want things in shades of gray because you are too weak and undisciplined to handle black and white, you've purchased the wrong book.

Bob Newman
San Juan del Norte
Mosquito Coast
Nicaragua

PART ONE:

Politics and the Radical Left

"In Italy for thirty years under the Borgias, they had warfare, terror, murder, bloodshed. They produced Michelangelo, Leonardo da Vinci, and the Renaissance. In Switzerland, they had brotherly love, five hundred years of democracy and peace, and what did they produce? The cuckoo clock."

—Orson Wells, *The Third Man*

"Never show your emotion; it reveals your weakness. Never hate your enemy; it effects your judgment."

—Mario Puzo character Michael Corleone

Hate, Violence, and the Liberal Way

They are among the most hypocritical, hateful, and violent of people, yet they see themselves as being honest, kind, and peaceful. Anyone who understands English knows better.

As a lad growing up in Thomaston, Maine, in the 1960s, I loved studying myths and legends and was always interested in learning facts about those myths and legends of which most people were unaware. So you can imagine my amusement each time liberals show America what they are really about, which so often these days are hate, violence, and the damaging of the Bill of Rights and Constitution in general, with free speech being a prime target within the latter. It wasn't that long ago that liberals were believed to be nonviolent defenders of the Constitution who shunned hate.

Today the tiger's stripes are in full view.

Liberals cringe when they think of Iraqis enjoying freedoms they didn't have just over two years ago, and they become angry when the news reports a major reduction of attacks on U.S. troops along with a corresponding reduction of casualties. Liberals did not want the Bush doctrine to succeed, especially in the Middle East where most of the people are brown-skinned Muslims. As freedom spreads through the region, liberals grimace and curse as conservatives point to democracy marching into lands where once tyranny was pandemic. And liberals know that the more freedom spreads in the Middle East and elsewhere in Asia, the more the liberal message of oftentimes race-based hate and violence will be called into question by Americans who are seeing the left in its true light. Arabs with rights are a liberal's worst nightmare.

More and more Americans are recognizing the real left and the violent, hateful liberals who make it up. In Denver recently, three leftists who were about to attempt to strip President Bush of his right to free speech were caught before they could carry out their plan of disrupting a gathering of people who had come to hear the president speak. The liberals were ejected from the event and are now angry that they were caught and prevented from violating the First Amendment rights of a fellow American. The leftist *Denver Post* is calling for the heads of the Republicans who caught the hate mongers before their anti-First Amendment plan could be put into action. Incredibly, the fish-wrap daily says it was wrong for someone to have prevented the leftists from preventing a conservative American from exercising his free-speech rights.

Can you say "irony" right after you say "hypocrisy?"

The liberals, encouraged by the notoriety their Marxist poster boy Ward Churchill has garnered of late, have now taken to threatening and physically attacking conservative speakers like Ann Coulter, Bill Kristol, David Horowitz, et al. This is classic liberal hate, whose manifesto calls for assaulting those with whom they disagree. Last night, Alan Colmes of FOX News Channel's "Hannity & Colmes," joked at how Horowitz was assaulted by a liberal at a recent college speech.

Although I am now quite nonviolent (I haven't beaten anyone up in about a decade), I know that, because of my previous life as a Marine for 20 years on active duty, such an attack on me while giving a speech would instantly result in my liberal would-be assailant waking up in a coma. I, for one, will not allow myself to be assaulted by anyone, as I have both a legal right and moral obligation to defend myself, and said defense will not be with a chocolate-cream pie but a rapid combo of flailing limbs and appendages. Rather than run off or just take the hit, I encourage all conservatives to vigorously defend themselves against anyone who assaults them.

What is especially entertaining is how the liberals will now decry my promise to defend myself against them.

There's that "irony" word again.

Will the Real Dick Clarke Please Stand Up?

One of the points in my "10-Point Plan to Win the War on Terror" is the Government Employee Accountability Act, which, if written and signed into law, would hold incompetent, negligent buffoons like Richard Clarke fully accountable for their shortcomings, failures, and dereliction of duty.

I love a parade, and this week's parade before the mostly career politicians on the so-called 9-11 Commission was quite a sight. The most intriguing of the guests was chameleon-man Richard "Dirty Dick" Clarke.

Dick, who is praised as a demigod by most Democrats because of his slanderous and almost wholly unsupported attack on his most recent boss, George Bush, was called on the carpet by former U.S. Navy Secretary John Lehman, who said the one-time counterterrorism czar had a serious credibility problem. But it wasn't just Lehman who took Dirty Dick to task, for many unaligned reporters, as well as those with a usually clear-cut agenda to influence rather than inform, dug into the facts of the matter as they pertain to a man many say was looking not only to sell books but wrangle the job of Secretary of Homeland Security if war-hero-turned-Viet-Cong-hugging socialist John Kerry managed to get into the White House.

Dirty Dick, whose long list of graphic failures include the 1993 bombing of the World Trade Center, 1993 loss of 18 U.S. Army Rangers and Delta Force commandos in Somalia, 1996 missed capture/shoot-down of Osama bin Laden as he flew from Sudan to Pakistan, 1996 bombing of Khobar Towers that killed 19 Americans, 1998 bombings of the U.S. Embassies in Kenya and Tanzania, 2000 near-sinking of the USS *Cole* that killed 17 sailors, and 2001 terrorist attacks on the World Trade Center and Pentagon, says all this was mostly the fault of other people, even though he was the lead "expert" responsible for helping to make sure such things as the aforementioned didn't happen.

Oh, sure, he put on a good act before the commission, saying "I failed you," but that transparent mea culpa shtick doesn't pass muster among those who know propaganda when they see, hear, and smell it. He was going for the sympathy vote, and I for one was not surprised when Clarke's groupie schmucks ran to hug and kiss him after his bogus display of emotion.

Clarke had three clear goals: (1) sell as many books as possible, (2) talk enough trash to seriously boost what he can charge for speeches and personal appearances, and (3) secure the position of Secretary of Homeland Security had John Kerry been elected. (Can you imagine the howling rage this loser let loose when he learned that Tom Ridge was being offered that position instead of him?)

Clarke is on record as time and again singing the praises of the Bush Administration's approach to the war on terror and counterterrorism. But then he came out for revenge and spun his earlier assessment of President Bush, the president's people, and the president's policies so he could enrich himself and extract his pound of flesh.

Clarke was right about one thing: he failed our country time after time after time after time after time after time after time. Sadly, instead of being held accountable, he got rich.

Sleep well, Dick, as your head rests on the graves of thousands of Americans you failed to protect.

Why the 9-11 Commission Was Doomed to Failure

It should be a national scandal as to why Congress has not commenced a thorough investigation into the so-called 9-11 Commission. The treachery, partisan chicanery, incompetence, and general dereliction of duty add up to a national disgrace. Here's why.

When the National Commission on Terrorist Attacks Upon the United States, more often called the 9-11 Commission, was created and I first read the names, affiliations, and lack of qualifications of its members, I instantly knew the commission would fail.

Instead of staffing the commission with seasoned, bona fide intelligence experts who would know where to look and what stones to turn over in determining what went wrong on 9-11, politicians and lawyers were appointed, some of whom had disgustingly clear personal and professional agendas. Such people have no interest in learning the truth and serving the nation. Their only interest lies in furthering their own careers, settling vendettas, gaining political ground, and making money by going on the speaking circuit, etc.

When national security advisor Condi Rice appeared before the commission, I wasn't the least bit surprised to see

Democratic Party hit man and mouthpiece Richard Ben-Veniste take up an outrageously prosecutorial tone in a grandstanding piece of showmanship that will go down in the annals of American history as one of the most callous, reckless, partisan stunts of the era. But it did my heart good to see Dr. Rice stand her ground with this arrogant swine. His blatant attempts at intimidation failed miserably, and he was therefore denied his goal of manipulating Dr. Rice's answers. The fact that Rice is African-American female must have felt like salt in his wounds.

Former Senator Bob Kerrey, a Medal of Honor recipient and former Navy SEAL platoon commander who admitted, a few years ago, to being a mass murderer (he admitted to committing and ordering horrific war crimes against unarmed civilians), tried to trip up Dr. Rice. He failed as well, and it was great to see Dr. Rice, who had done her homework, humiliate Kerrey by citing his insistence after the 2000 bombing of the USS *Cole* in Yemen that the United States kill Saddam Hussein because, as Kerrey wrongly believed, the Iraqi dictator was behind the attack (it was al Qaeda, not Saddam). Kerrey turned bright red, stammered and sputtered, and I loved it.

Back in the 1990s, Jamie Gorelick was a bureaucrat who was instrumental in preventing the Central Intelligence Agency and Federal Bureau of Investigation from sharing crucial intelligence on terrorist activity. On the 9-11 Commission she was investigating herself, which was a clear conflict of interest, but she refused to resign.

And Chairman Thomas Kean, when asked why he didn't have a problem with this conflict of interest and serious breach of ethics, said, "People ought to stay out of our business." This pompous statement is indicative of a man who failed to understand or simply did not care that the business he was conducting *was* the people's business. Everything he thought, said, or did in relation to the commission was the business of every U.S. citizen. For him to have said it wasn't revealed a power-mad, egotistical politician who should have been immediately fired.

Little of tangible substance came from the commission's final report, of course. The politicians and pettifoggers who made up the commission saw to its failure.

Talk Radio: Journalism or–or What?

A few years ago, I won a national-level Edward R. Murrow Award for investigative reporting. I received that award while my primary employment was that of a radio talk-show host on Newsradio 850 KOA in Denver. This little tidbit must crush Jason Salzman of the Rocky Mountain News, *who says talk radio isn't journalism.*

I had never heard of Jason Salzman until the morning of Saturday, May 28, 2005.

I was running a swab through the bore of my Prairie Arms-built .220 Swift varmint rifle (named the "Gunny Bob Varmint Exploder" at Prairie Arms, where the beast was constructed by "The Doctor" and his henchmen) at 0520 (5:20 AM), getting ready for a Memorial Day prairie dog shoot with "The Doctor" and two of his cohorts on the plains of eastern Colorado, when I forced my computer to visit the *Rocky Mountain News'* website. In doing so, I stumbled across a column by the aforementioned Mr. Salzman after I clicked on "Opinion" on the site's front page. Mr. Salzman's column that day had a title that said undercover media work was ethically shaky.

I was intrigued.

I clicked on the column.

Moments later I was laughing out loud (and annoying my cat, Squeaky, who was trying to sleep on my lap, and clearly bothering my parakeets, Ren and Stimpy) and thanking this columnist for handing me a great topic for my shows. His words were so amusing and thought-provoking that I momentarily stopped cleaning and stroking my weapon and started checking around for information on this Salzman fellow.

I was not to be disappointed.

In Mr. Salzman's column, he wrote in bold that "Talk radio is entertainment, not journalism."

Okay, I thought, *let's hear it.*

Mr. Salzman wrote that a supposed recent topic on a KHOW talk show was first covered in a *Rocky Mountain News* article.

Boy, there's a shocker. Talk radio covering a subject that print media is also covering.

Great flying frijoles! Two media mediums discussing the same topic. Diabolical! Imagine the global repercussions if the "NBC Nightly News" covered the same topic as the *New York Times* on the same day.

Mr. Salzman went on: "Callers are angry on talk radio all the time."

Gee, really?

Mr. Salzman was implying, of course, that readers of the *Rocky Mountain News* are never angry.

That's odd, because every day in the "Letters to the Editor" section of the *News,* readers write in to say how angry they are.

Must be some kind of a mix-up.

Why is it journalism if a consumer writes about his feelings regarding a particular story but it is not journalism if a consumer states his feelings on the air? I assume Mr.

Salzman believes that when two people on a television news show disagree, that show is no longer journalism.

Mr. Salzman continued: "Serious journalists should rarely care about the latest outrage on talk radio."

That's funny. If what Mr. Salzman says is true, then why, I wondered, is he writing about the latest outrage on talk radio? I guess he must not be a serious journalist. How does he not understand that most topics on talk radio are the same topics written about in his newspaper? And why doesn't he know that Denver talk-radio hosts are frequently written about by other journalists in his paper? Why does he feel that newspaper journalists who write about us are not serious, which as I just pointed out, includes himself?

Mr. Salzman closed that section of his column by saying, "The talk radio medium does not represent the pulse of the people by any stretch of the imagination."

He offers no evidence whatsoever to back up this claim (that's because there is no evidence available to support his bizarre claim, which is demonstrably false, of course) and does not explain why his newspaper's circulation continues to plummet, nor does he explain why talk-radio shows like the "Gunny Bob Show" are so popular.

Mr. Salzman is transparent in this. He doesn't like talk radio because it is dominated by conservative talk-show hosts such as myself. If it were dominated by leftists, he would never have said the things he said.

But we must go back to Mr. Salzman's premise that talk radio is not journalism.

The question must be asked: "What is journalism?"

If an on-air media employee becomes a highly successful broadcast and print military and terrorism analyst, but that person derives his primary income from talk-radio shows, does that mean he is not a journalist?

According to Mr. Salzman, yes, even if that person has

authored 20 books (none by "vanity" publishers) and more than 2,000 articles and columns. (I could write as a small child and was recognized for this skill by my teachers, but the Corps gets most of the credit for my accomplishments, not me.) Mr. Salzman must hate the idea that, on talk radio in less than four years, I've broken many stories and made dozens of accurate assessments and predictions in the war on terror. For some reason, breaking major news stories and making dead-on assessments and predictions in the war on terror on talk radio doesn't qualify as journalism. However, had he been able to do the same in his newspaper, he would have considered it journalism.

I dug just a tad deeper, which was as easy as typing "Jason Salzman" into Google.

Mr. Salzman brags about being a "senior manager for Greenpeace USA."

Great.

No, seriously. I don't like the idea of whales getting harpooned in the back either. I applaud Mr. Salzman for being part of Greenpeace and trust he has plenty of video of himself in a Zodiac between an in-flight harpoon and a whale.

I was not surprised to find that Mr. Salzman is a hero of Communist Party USA.

Yes, Mr. Salzman complains bitterly on that organization's website (www.cpusa.org) that America had the gall, the nerve, the unmitigated audacity to free the people of Afghanistan from the Taliban.

What did he have to say to his presumably fellow communists?

How about this: "Americans might well appreciate being given the opportunity to consider for themselves what bin Laden and serious opponents [such as North Korea] of the Afghan war have to say."

Funny how Mr. Salzman somehow missed the fact that

when women openly disagreed with the Taliban and bin Laden, or violated their rules, they got a bullet through the head on a soccer field now being used by kids playing soccer.

Does Mr. Salzman have a problem with women who want civil rights, including the right not to be shot in the head?

And Mr. Salzman's apparent hero, Osama bin Laden, is on videotape admitting to the premeditated murder of nearly 3,000 Americans on 9-11-2001. But Salzman implies we should listen to bin Laden because bin Laden is right.

Does Mr. Salzman also feel that Joe Stalin was a great man who should have also been listened to more closely? Mr. Salzman probably gets teary eyed when he thinks about the long-gone *gulag* where more than 1,000,000 people died gruesome deaths on orders from Stalin, another of Mr. Salzman's idols.

Mr. Salzman continues on the Communist Party USA website: "Opponents of the Afghan war are not limited to anti-war freaks and celebrities. As Phil Donahue has noted, there are plenty of credible people willing to speak out . . ."

But, as expected, Mr. Salzman cites none of these "plenty of credible people" on the Communist Party USA website. And Phil Donahue, an apparent mentor of Mr. Salzman, is clearly an expert in terrorism, jihad, and al Qaeda. After all, he's from Hollywood and used to have a talk show on television. I do not know why Mr. Salzman respects television talk shows but not radio talk shows.

I was also not surprised to see that Mr. Salzman writes for *People's Weekly World*, an online newspaper that by its own admission acts as a mouthpiece for Communist Party USA and whose stated goal it is to champion the ideals and goals of "Marxism and socialism." As you may know, one of the primary goals of Marxism is the elimination of all civil and human rights, as we saw accomplished so handily by Lenin, Stalin, Kruschev, Breshnev, and other murderous

Soviet leaders. Mr. Salzman must have loved those guys.

But in what may be Mr. Salzman's weirdest claim, he states in an "On The Media" column that "according to the Society of Professional Journalists and journalistic standards that are widely accepted," topics like "crime and disaster" are "not news."

Huh?

The answer to the riddle of Mr. Salzman is, in the end, quite a simple one.

Envy.

Mr. Salzman knows people like me and other popular talk-show hosts are relied upon for news, information, and opinion far more than he. This troubles him greatly, just as the demise of the Soviet Union, the sacking of the Taliban, and the fall of Saddam Hussein trouble him. Tyranny is on the wane, and Mr. Salzman frets that the march of freedom into regions and countries long ruled by brutal dictators may topple the dwindling number of remaining tyrants he so worships. As he longs for the days of Pol Pot, Idi Amin, Stalin, Hitler, Mao, and the Taliban, he looks to North Korea, Iran, Cuba, Syria, and Zimbabwe and wonders with trepidation and fear how much longer these regimes can survive.

Freedom is coming to the world, Mr. Salzman, and there's little you and your friends in Communist Party USA or al Qaeda can do about it. Even if your pals resort to terrorism here in the homeland again, we will defeat them. You loathe those whose opinions differ from yours, and your fury boils over when those opinions are heard in a medium more trusted than yours.

But now we know all about you, Mr. Salzman, and we thank you for a great talk-radio topic!

The Perfect Automatons

Mike Rosen, host of the "Mike Rosen Show" on Newsradio 850 KOA and my colleague, received from a high school student a remarkable MP3 of one of the student's teachers delivering an anti-freedom political indoctrination speech to students in what was supposed to be a world geography class. The rest is history.

Listening to the high school teacher's indoctrination session, I was swept back into the 1980s and in my mind's eye could see myself standing before the huddled, dazed, half frozen students deep in the forested mountains of Maine aboard the U.S. Navy's remote and secretive Redington Training Facility. My uniform hat was adorned with a red and gold crest, in the middle of which was the hammer and sickle of the Soviet Union. Thinking for a moment at the time that I was a Marine Corps gunnery sergeant, I considered how odd a job I had at the moment, playing the part of a communist military officer.

I was giving an indoctrination speech at one of the four Department of Defense Survival-Evasion-Resistance-Escape (SERE) schools, using classic propaganda as a means by which I hoped to achieve my goal of convincing some of the students that America was the aggressor in the Cold War and was an evil nation that had committed a great deal of genocide and other forms of hideous abuse on the poorer peoples of the world.

Returning to March 2006 and the comfortable confines of my library, I noted how Jay Bennish, a supposed geography teacher at Overland High School in Aurora, Colorado, was using precisely the same indoctrination techniques on his students that I used nearly 20 years earlier, except I was teaching my students how to recognize and defend against propaganda as a tool of indoctrination, whereas Bennish was using the techniques to actually indoctrinate his students. Speaking as if what he was saying were undeniable facts, he accosted his students with demonstrable falsehoods, half truths, misinformation, disinformation, and a smattering of truth to work over his mostly hapless charges.

But a noted difference was how I was feeling sorry for Bennish's students and had not felt sorry for mine.

Why?

My students were in the practical application and testing phase of their training. They had already been taught how to recognize indoctrination techniques and were now expected to use those skills to defend themselves against this insidious process, which American military men first experienced as prisoners of war during the Korean War. And they were men, not children.

Conversely, Bennish's students have not been trained to recognize the ruse and have not been given tools and techniques to ward off the tactic. Defenseless, most would be putty in the man's hands. And they are children who tend to be naturally rebellious and believe anything their teacher says because they are taught from Day One that the teacher is always right. Perfect victims, in other words, which was what Bennish was counting on.

On the "Gunny Bob Show," students at Overland High

School and teachers there and at other schools called in to say how such goings on are commonplace in our schools. One teacher told of another teacher who attempts to indoctrinate his third-grade class with leftist thought.

Sean Allen, the student in Bennish's world geography class who recorded the anti-America rant, said on FOX News Channel that Bennish's class consists of 20 percent geography and 80 percent Bennish's political opinions.

When I interviewed Cherry Creek School District public information officer (PIO) Tustin Amole, she assured me that the schools monitor classrooms and teachers to make sure they are teaching properly, sticking to the approved syllabus, and not abusing their students. But she also said, "We can't fix what we don't know is broken."

If the teachers were in fact being effectively monitored, the district would have known what Bennish was up to. The reality of the situation is that teachers are not being effectively monitored and now the district is scrambling for cover.

As expected, a *Denver Post* editorial lavished praise on Bennish. Would the paper have done this had Bennish been ranting that had Christianity been successful in spreading through the Middle East and displacing Islam, the region would not be in as much turmoil? (A silly notion.) No. The *Post* would have seen it differently and been calling for Bennish's head on a pike in the middle of the ACLU's front lawn. The editorial intentionally and transparently failed to mention that the many claims of fact Bennish made are easily proved false, such as:

1. The United States uses chemical weapons in Bolivia and Peru
2. Bolivians and Peruvians do not use coca
3. The U.S. is the world's largest producer of tobacco products

4. The U.S. sold tanks, planes, and guns to Iran and Iraq during their war
5. North Carolina produces most of the tobacco in the United States
6. Millions and millions of Chinese, Iranians, and Peruvians die each year of tobacco-related illnesses
7. The U.S. killed 75 innocent Pakistanis in a missile attack
8. The U.S. perpetrated 7,000 terrorists attacks in Cuba between 1960–1962, killing thousands of people
9. The U.S. killed thousands of Afghan and Sudan citizens in missile attacks in the 1990s

Why didn't the *Post* mention these lies? Because the *Post* didn't want you to know about them. The *Post* wanted to deceive you with a lie of omission and misdirected emphasis. (The *Post* hates it when I dismantle their arguments and reveal their complicity in the lies of leftists, and the *Post*'s editorial board has refused to accept my offer to debate the entire board simultaneously. Go figure.)

I have offered to give a fair and balanced, 20-question world geography test, using the course's stated standards, to the students in Bennish's class to determine what the class really knows about the topic, but the Cherry Creek School District will not allow me to do so, even though I am certified in Instructional System Design (ISD) and have 10 years of formal teaching experience.

The children are not to blame here because as such, most don't know any better. Bennish, his alleged supervisors at Overland High School, and Dr. Monte C. Moses, superintendent of Cherry Creek School District, are responsible for this abusive outrage. Overland High school principal Jana Frieler demonstrated reprehensible dereliction of duty in allowing Bennish to get away with such disgusting behavior. Moses failed to make sure Freiler was doing her job. The total lack of leadership demonstrated by Moses and Freiler reveals two people in charge who couldn't lead a Marine private to a free six-pack of Coors Light.

And all the while, the children pay the price as Bennish builds his radical's resumé.

A Darwinian Dilemma: Societal De-Evolution

History is replete with examples of how nations come and nations go. How and when America will cease to exist as the nation it is now, no one knows. However, there are hints.

As a boy in single digits growing up in part in southern rural Florida in the 1960s, I would spend hours watching the myriad critters that called the Everglades, Lake Okeechobee, and the warren of canals in that part of the state home. The creatures my eyes surveilled were many and diverse, and I paid special attention to how each animal had adapted to its environment.

The anhinga, a.k.a. water turkey and snake bird, would dive under water and catch bream with its beak, with which it would then surface, toss into the air, and swallow head first so the dorsal spines of the fish did not jam in the bird's throat.

From underwater, the alligator would quietly sneak up on a log crammed with napping turtles and then lunge at one from below, the loud snapping and crunching of the turtle's shell telling the tale of life and death.

And the manatee, or sea cow, would casually gobble water hyacinth as it used its broad tail to slowly maneuver beneath the tasty plants that had been imported into Florida from South America, likely during the 1884 Cotton States Exposition in New Orleans.

I had no idea, though, after reading Darwin's *The Origin of Species* for the first time, that successful societies evolve in a manner similar to species. Later in life, after reading a great deal of history and after visiting 40-some-odd countries on every continent that has countries, I would recognize this fact and would come to know that no society is immune to this phenomenon. But in the case of societies, some actually de-evolve, meaning they once had the ability to adapt to changes but later lost that ability.

Enter societal evolutionary factors al Qaeda, Ward Churchill, and the Churchill cult.

Unlike the nearly four years following the Japanese attack on Pearl Harbor and other Hawaiian targets, it took America only a few months to turn on itself after the attacks of 9-11. Even years after World War II ended, Americans were still pretty tight as a nation and could easily understand threats when they popped up.

That began to change (read: the nation began to de-evolve) in the 1960s, when Americans began to be unable or unwilling to recognize the importance of stemming threats to democracy abroad before those threats arrived on our shores. But by December 2001, America as a whole, despite the worst attack on them in history, could not or would not grasp the nature of that which threatens to this day its very survival.

Global asymmetric warfare against Muslim terrorists may be too complicated and too unsettling a concept for us to effectively adapt to as a people. And as Darwin told us, those who fail to adapt, die.

Like the Roman Empire, arrogance is perhaps the foremost factor working towards the demise of America.

Many Americans don't believe America could succumb to Islamic terrorism.

Following arrogance is liberal hatred for those who are willing and even anxious to defend the very principles that make liberalism possible.

Self-loathing is next, with the blame-America-first faction (Ward Churchill, Ted Kennedy, John Kerry, Howard Dean, Robert Byrd, et al) telling us that America had it coming because of its desire to see freedom spread to people other than the lily white.

Finally we have pure ignorance. Many Americans do not understand that the First Amendment does not overrule laws like Sections 2381 (treason) and 2385 (advocating the overthrow of the government) of Title 18 of the United States Code. Ward Churchill's acts may be treasonous (they aid and comfort the enemy) and he publicly advocates the overthrow of the government and total destruction of America. We have his words to these ends on tape and in writing.

Now 200 of Churchill's hate-filled sycophants—all University of Colorado faculty members—are demanding in a full-page newspaper ad that the investigation into their hate-mongering god's pro-terrorism anti-American activities be terminated.

The dodo became extinct when it could not deal with new threats to its existence. A mere 81 years passed from the time those threats were introduced to the dodo's habitat to the day the last of the dodos walked in the denuded forests of Mauritius.

There's a movement afoot among liberals to change our national bird to the dodo.

Who among us will stop them?

Reveling In My Abnormality

Remarkably talented in the realm of hating America first, infamous Denver Post *columnist Reggie Rivers never fails to amuse, annoy, mislead, and misinform.*

I am abnormal and wish to explain.

I am abnormal, according to leftist extremist Reggie Rivers, who writes a column in the *Denver Post,* because I believe in defending (and have defended with my life, as have millions more true Americans) the flag which represents the principles for which so many Americans have died.

Frankly, I am proud to be so abnormal.

In his latest anti-American tirade in the way-to-the-left *Post,* "Radical Reggie" continues his never-ending attacks on America by stating that "the flag is not without its problems." People like Osama bin Laden love it when Americans attack their own flag and all it means, but this fact doesn't bother Reg one iota.

Reg says the flag is "merely a symbol of our ideals . . ." and therefore isn't all that important. Tell me, Reg, do you have any of the trophies and other stuff you won while playing for the Broncos and in college and high school? You do? Those are mere symbols, Reg. So why do you keep and treasure them? Why not burn them as you say the flag should be burned?

The former Bronco goes on to say that anyone who respects the flag is participating in "idol worship" and is therefore violating the Second Commandment.

No, I am not making this up.

Finally, Radical Reggie says that references to the flag in our national anthem are about as meaningful as "Britney Spears."

I wonder if Reggie is troubled at all that terrorists around the world cheer him on when he gets going on his anti-American rants?

People like Reggie can't understand the importance of symbols in our lives, which become valuable because of the blood and lives sacrificed for what a symbol like the flag represents. Reg can't grasp this concept because he has never risked anything for anyone, having spent his entire adult life ensconced in wealth brought to him by his career in professional football. While he played games for a living and was (and still is) living large in luxury and safety, Americans willing to die so that Reggie can continue that Bohemian lifestyle are bleeding and dying on battlefields hither and yon. It is highly doubtful that a single one of those men and women Reggie belittles, mocks, and insults could be named by the former Bronco-turned-novelist.

At the end of the day, Reggie has done nothing of genuine consequence in his life and is so troubled by this fact that he feels he must snipe at those who have from the lair that is his *Post* column. His repeated claims to be a patriotic American ring hollow, for true patriotism isn't demonstrated by cheap words on fish wrap. It is demonstrated by deeds. But the self-righteous have always been wont to crow from their perches about how much they love their country while others do the nation's oftentimes deadly dirty work under conditions people like Reggie can't even imagine.

Words are cheap. Blood, limbs, eyes, entrails, and lives are expensive, and those are things Reggie and his ilk steadfastly refuse to risk so that others might live in freedom.

To borrow from today's American lexicon, there are those who love to loudly talk the talk but who never walk the walk because only their freedom is important to them, whereas the freedom of others, especially Third World Muslims, is of no concern to them whatsoever. Knowing this and feeling unworthy because of that knowledge, they use verbal arrows to pierce the symbols of those willing to put their money where their mouth is.

But we're used to it, Reg, so fire away. When all is said and done, we sleep with clear consciences in knowing that our deeds will forever drown out your vile, hateful words.

Hate Goes Out of Style

I am amused by the myth that says liberals are tolerant. To counter this ridiculous notion, I have a marvelous collection of e-mails and blog entries from liberals who disagree with some of my political views and want me and my family dead because of it. Much of this intolerance, hatred, and violent rhetoric towards me is generated by the leftist radio mob known as Air America, where I am reviled, which means I am doing my job.

As usual, it was nearly impossible for listeners' calls to get through on my radio shows the day after the 2004 presidential and congressional elections, as callers on both sides of the passageway and those in the middle queued up to analyze and comment on the results. Callers from Missouri and Texas to Colorado and California and many places between weighed in. The overriding consensus? The politics of hate are unacceptable, and the result of the extremism controlling the Democratic Party was the loud crack of a bitch-slapping by mainstream America.

But it wasn't just the politics of hate that sounded so sour a note in my audience's ears. It was the politics of lies, distortions, fear, racial division, and intolerance that devastated the once-respected and even honorable party of

Franklin Delano Roosevelt and John F. Kennedy. So now the question is: will the ruinous leaders of the Democratic Party—Kennedy, Pelosi, Gore, McAuliffe, Kerry, Carter, Graham, and the like—be allowed to continue on the destructive path, or will they be sent packing down the path of political irrelevance to join Tom Daschle in the malodorous scrap heap of hate?

And what of the oftentimes (but not always) leftist media? The *New York Times*, CBS, NBC, ABC, *Los Angeles Times*, *Boston Globe*, *San Francisco Chronicle*, *Denver Post*, and like-minded media acted as fire support for the deranged Democrats. The distortions and outright lies these outfits employed in their failed attempts to influence their respective audiences rather than inform them has rightfully cast a shadow over media that truly believes most Americans are easily manipulated morons who are too dim to figure things out on their own. Despite pulling every dirty trick in the book, the leftist media failed and now despise the average American all the more. If my audience is any indication, most Americans are anything but mindless dolts who rely upon Bruce Springsteen, Alec Baldwin, Robert Redford, Michael Moore, Whoopi Goldberg (Kerry said her now infamous hate speech at Radio City Music Hall represented the "heart and soul" of America), Barbra Streisand, Sheryl Crow, the Dixie Chicks, Al Franken, Sean Penn, and Susan Sarandon for political wisdom. Which political geniuses within the Democratic Party decided that the shrill opinions of Left Coasters from Hollywood, ensconced in their Malibu beach houses and Beverly Hills mansions, would hold sway over the majority of Americans, remains a mystery. And deranged billionaire financier George Soros isn't exactly an endearing figure to most Americans. Amusingly, it was pathetic riffraff like Moore and Franken, with their repugnant hatemongering, who opened America's eyes as to what the Democratic Party has become.

But perhaps the biggest question is why Democrats thought a socialist Massachusetts (read: Yankee) senator with a penchant for bragging about his medals (a cardinal sin to professional military men) and a billionaire wife could win the presidency while we are at war. It is blatantly clear that the wiser choice would have been a moderate Southerner. You tell me who worked out better for the Dems: Dukakis (liberal Yankee from Taxachusetts) or Clinton (moderate Southerner).

So now the "soul searching" continues among the maimed and dazed Democrats. Totally bereft of ethical leadership, their ship will continue to drift aimlessly with the tide, their listing vessel becalmed under the broiling sun of scrutiny and the ship's wheel clutched in the dainty hands of extremist Howard Dean. Their stores running perilously low, the crew has already set upon themselves in a frenzy of cannibalism brought on by frantic, angry accusations of incompetence. Could they look aft, they would see the discarded carcass of perhaps the one man who might have saved them.

Aye, Captain Lieberman. You were a good and decent man. T'is a shame the scurvy dogs had you walk the plank so early in the voyage.

The Imaginary Constitution of the Radical Left

Some self-proclaimed experts on the Constitution of the United States have apparently never read it. However, don't think for a moment that a little thing like not having read the Constitution might stop them from expounding at great length upon it.

It has been my great good fortune to have held some fascinating jobs; billets that have allowed me to learn and do things most Americans never have the opportunity to learn or do. I've been allowed to lead Marines in combat; teach advanced evasion, wilderness survival, interrogation resistance, and prison-escape methods to elite military personnel; instruct various people in counterterrorism measures; and teach those with the need to know how to recognize and defend against propaganda. I have indeed been lucky in my job assignments. And my job today as the host of a rather popular talk-radio program is one I enjoy for a variety of reasons, including my being required to do a lot of research on the broad array of topics I cover on the "Gunny Bob Show."

Politics is a frequent topic on my show, as you might imagine, and for each three-hour show I average around eight hours of show-preparation time. Having done hundreds and hundreds of shows on politics, for which I have read and reread the Constitution many times and interviewed many Constitutional scholars in the course of said research, I was confident, until this morning, that my take on, and knowledge of, the Constitution was above average. But I still manage to learn new things about the Constitution.

For example, today I learned that the Constitution requires "the media," "the courts" and "international organizations" (such as the United Nations, European Union, International Criminal Court, Human Rights Watch, and Amnesty International, presumably) to closely supervise the president of the United States, a.k.a. the commander in chief of the U.S. armed forces, including during time of war. In all my research of the Constitution, how could I have missed that?

And the same sage from whom I learned these facts caused me to be mortified yet again when he informed me that a commander in chief who takes secrecy seriously during time of war is clearly an evil tyrant. How embarrassing for me to learn after all the time I spent in the field of counterterrorism, reconnaissance, and special operations that secrecy is a silly idea and that we should tell our enemy what we are doing and how we are doing it. D'oh!

Who is this Constitutional scholar, sagacious warfighting strategist, and intelligence guru?

Why, none other than *Denver Post* columnist Reggie Rivers, who used to play football (yes, that is his sole qualification to be a political, warfare, Constitutional and legal columnist for the notorious daily).

From his fetid lair protected by a parapet of the far-left fringe, Rivers mounts his assault on the facts. A vulnerable public, most of whom have never read the Constitution and most of whom have never been taught how to recognize the false implications, half-truths, misinformation, and disinformation that form the foundation of Rivers' blatantly leftist propaganda (much less defend against such perfidious attacks), is left to sort through the shattered remnants of the truth.

That's where I come in. Because the "Gunny Bob Show" is heard by far, far more people than Rivers has readers, and because of my real-world (as opposed to entirely academic, vicarious, and theoretical) background, I am able to point out Rivers' duplicitous claims and illusory rhetoric.

Of course, Rivers' asinine declaration that the media, international organizations, and the courts are required by the Constitution to supervise the commander in chief is demonstrably false. As most high school sophomores can tell you with certainty, the Constitution says no such thing. Still, Rivers assumes his readers are so moronic that they will accept him at his specious word. Rivers' admirers remind me of the herd of Cornish sheep I watched one day in Tregony as the leader gathered his herd into the corner of a rock-walled glen, allowing a pair of foxes to pick off several lambs in under a minute with ease, knowing the sheep would all cower there. In the three minutes it took me to cover the half mile between me and the sheep, the foxes had slain five lambs.

Looking at the herd's dominant ram, I wondered how so inept a leader had managed to gain a purchase on power.

Perhaps he used to play football.

Rebel Without a Clue

This chapter was almost too easy to write, given the subject's transparent nature.

Indeed, a picture tells a thousand words, but words tell far more.

The notorious *Denver Post*'s latest ugly attempt to chip away at the new-born, still-tenuous freedom Iraqis have obtained recently manifested itself in a front-page, far-from-subtle screed about one Jeff Englehart, late of the United States Army.

Written by an easily manipulated reporter named Erin Emery infatuated with the self-styled rogue, the article is a study in pro-socialist propaganda dutifully recited by the would-be wild one.

I can see the problematic, undisciplined ex-soldier mugging in his bathroom mirror, emulating Marlon Brando's Johnny Strabler in *The Wild One*.

A girl asks the charismatic Strabler, "What're you rebelling against, Johnny?"

Responds Johnny, "What'd'ya got?"

Decorated with his dark-as-possible aviator-style shades and a disheveled, mop-top haircut, Englehart sneers at the mirror, snaps open a Zippo, and fires up another smoke.

The large, color photo of the hopeful provocateur caught my eye as I walked through the 850 KOA newsroom, the paper tossed on some filing cabinets. Glancing down and before reading the article's title or a single word in the piece, I knew precisely what I was looking at: the classic wannabe revolutionary frightened of the truth and desperate to be declared an enemy of the state, but knowing in the shallows of his soul that he will never grow beyond being just another puny fish in a sprawling sea of hate.

I caught myself grinning as I read the stickers on the top of his laptop, a sophomoric, predictable collection of leftist tripe: "Revolution begins with an individual," the mandatory peace symbol, some bombs falling amid the words "What would Jesus bomb?", a skull, a circled cross with a slash across it.

How trendy.

The article is even more revealing and illuminates a young man whose personal hero, Che Guevara, plays a critical part in the dim goings-on within Englehart's oh-so-angry brain-housing group. Here, the reporter's own inability (unwillingness?) to separate fact from fiction comes into play when Emery claims Guevara was murdered, when in reality the bloodthirsty terrorist who butchered scores in the name of Marx, Mao, and Castro was captured in battle by a Bolivian army unit and executed for his innumerable gruesome crimes. But why let facts get in the way of a romantic, anti-America tale with a local twist?

Guevara is certainly a telling roll model for our transparent young socialist.

He tells the laughable tale of how he intercepts a prospective recruit outside of a Marine Corps recruiting office. He claims the lad tells him he wants to join the

Marines so he can find out what it is like to kill a man. Englehart's fantasy response is to tell the kid that the so-called terrorists in Iraq are really just innocent farmers.

Innocent farmers who gleefully blow up children.

Englehart then regales the reporter with the story of how *Socialist Worker* published one of his anti-freedom rants while he was still in the army. He then claims he feared one or more of his fellow soldiers would kill him for his political views; the expected I-feared-for-my-life shtick. He recalls how his barracks room "was filled with anti-war books, socialist propaganda, anarchist literature, and posters" and that he, being a coward, quickly got rid of the material because his leaders were searching for evidence that would lead them to an anti-freedom protestor within their ranks. The *Post*'s enamored reporter sucks it up and skips the obvious next question: If you are so brave and committed to your politics, why didn't you have the moral courage, the intestinal fortitude, the guts to show your leaders how you really felt?

He goes on to brag how he was nearly court-martialed for his views. He tells how his lack of discipline allowed him to harm his unit's morale and therefore combat effectiveness. To him, this is a badge of honor. Again, no challenge from the reporter, who says Englehart is "an independent thinker."

Funny. I wasn't aware that socialists who toe the leftist line and have their opinions dictated to them by their masters were known as independent thinkers.

The reporter fails yet again to ask the obvious question: If you are so committed to your view that America was wrong to free the Iraqis and the terrorists are right to fight us, why haven't you joined al Qaeda in Iraq? Surely you would be a great asset to al-Zarqawi.

In the end, young Englehart yearns for an imaginary

socialist utopia with himself as ruler, a jaunty beret perched atop his head, a cigarette replacing his mentor's Cuban cigar.

Pedestrian.

Pedantic.

Pathetic.

Maniacal Media or Presidential Dereliction of Duty?

When one is angry, one has two basic choices: get over it or do something about it. I am waiting for President Bush to get deadly serious about leaks and top-secret documents regarding our war plans.

An angry President Bush said yesterday that it was illegal for the *New York Times* to have in its possession and publish top-secret intelligence on the National Security Agency's (NSA) orders from the president to conduct electronic surveillance of known al Qaeda operatives and supporters inside the United States, some of whom are American citizens. This report by the *Times* placed in jeopardy an unknown number of surveillance operations against al Qaeda and thus aided the enemy, who now know that they must flee or change their communications methods. Those terrorists now know that any plans they had in the works could very well have been compromised, making new plans mandatory, and when they begin making those new plans, you can bet your sweet bippie al Qaeda operatives here in the United States will use more secure means of communication than telephones and e-mails.

But I don't understand why the president is so upset.

The White House, Congress, and various agencies within our government are rife with criminals who, for personal, political, or financial reasons, enjoy stealing classified information and giving or selling it to a praetorian media, which then, in order to increase their profit margin, goes public with that classified intelligence, knowing full well that Americans might die because of the leak.

Profit far outweighs life and national security at the infamous *New York Times*, Mr. President, which you should have known.

It is a commonplace occurrence for the media to brag in public and report that they have illegally acquired oftentimes top-secret intelligence. I have personally filed reports with the FBI on this matter, detailing the likely whereabouts of such stolen intelligence and advised the FBI on how to retrieve that intelligence. I have demanded that the United States attorney general investigate and file charges against these media; possession of stolen, top-secret intelligence is a felony in this country, in case you were wondering.

President Bush has only himself and his administration to blame for this fiasco. The *New York Times* felt empowered to come into the possession of this extremely sensitive intelligence about a top-secret program for electronically surveilling terrorists right here at home, and because the Bush administration refuses to order the FBI to recover the intelligence documents and arrest the editor, publisher, reporters, and others involved, the media will continue to steal or possess classified intelligence from the United States government. Yet the president still complains bitterly about all these leaks and the *Times* damaging our national security and endangering our citizens.

President Bush is encouraging the theft, illegal dissemination, and illegal possession of highly classified intelligence because he hasn't even attempted to hold accountable the thieves who commit the crimes.

Where are the arrests? I am unaware of a single arrest in any of the thefts of such intelligence.

When the *Times* announced it was guilty of possessing stolen top-secret intelligence about an ongoing counterterrorism operation inside the United States, why didn't 500 FBI agents immediately descend upon the newspaper's offices to recover the intelligence and make arrests? Interrogations of the publisher, editors, reporters, and others who were involved in the plot may very well have revealed who illegally gave or sold the newspaper the intelligence.

The president and his administration should be dealing with the media just as previous administrations dealt with the Soviets, Chinese, Cubans, East Germans, North Koreans, and so on when it comes to espionage. Stealing, selling, transferring, possessing, and publishing top-secret intelligence that aids the enemy is a deadly serious federal offense, but the U.S. attorney general and FBI have done nothing to hold the criminals accountable, whether they are members of Congress, the NSA, or whomever. This *c'est la vie* attitude is why such destructive, extraordinarily dangerous activities by our media will continue unabated.

So until the president directs the U.S. attorney general and FBI to do their respective jobs, I don't want to hear him whining about top-secret counterterrorism operations being exposed by the media.

Michael Moore: Master Propagandist and Brilliant Pitchman

If Michael Moore is anything—some would say he is many things—he is an opportunist with a penchant for capitalism, this despite his public cries for socialism to come to America. People were still perishing from the effects of Hurricane Katrina and New Orleans Mayor Ray Nagin's fatally inept response when Moore decided to make some money off of the dead and dying.

Michael Moore, that bloated sack of leftist protoplasm who made scads of money on his masterfully misleading *Bowling for Columbine*, was all over the television and Internet, whining like the loser slob he is because Disney said it would not distribute his new project, *Fahrenheit 9/11*. (The film wants you to believe George Bush and the Republican Party are in cahoots with Osama bin Laden and his family and that the attacks of 9/11 were all part of that vast right-wing conspiracy. No, really.) Disney did not want to upset its customers with more bogus garbage from a socialist rabble-rouser, which Disney said might cost the company customers in the long run. Moore and his mindless minions say it was censorship and a conspiracy between conservatives and Disney.

Disney in a conspiracy with conservatives. The company that is so proud of its "Gay Day" at Walt Disney World.

Right.

Moore, a master propagandist equal in skill to Leni Riefenstahl, [1] is a shrewd and brilliant marketing expert who knows how to make money by plugging his films as being controversial and way to the left. This whole thing, of course, was a setup by Moore to sell his film (which easily got a distributor) like hotcakes before the November presidential election. He admitted that it was crucial for him to get his film distributed before November so he could further galvanize the radical, screaming, wacko left against George Bush and his fight to defend this nation in the war on terror.

Moore, who gloated on his website that the Cannes Film Festival was to show his new "documentary," says: "The non-fiction film revolution rolls on!"

The very idea of a Michael Moore "documentary" being nonfiction is absurd. True documentaries are factual works meant to inform. Moore's films are deceitful works that blend some facts with half-truths, lies, innuendo, misinformation, and disinformation in order to influence rather than inform a gullible audience.

Blowhard Moore says this is all about censorship, too. Hey, Bluto: corporations are not bound by law to assist you in speaking your mind. It is up to you and those who blindly follow you down the treacherous path of hatred and lies you have chosen to spread your vile message.

Moore says Disney refused to distribute his film because Florida Governor Jeb Bush would have held back critical tax breaks to Disney if he did so. This is ridiculous because the governor of Florida has absolutely no control over who gets what tax breaks. Florida tax laws, passed by the Florida legislature, do that.

1. Hitler's infamous propaganda filmmaker.

Moore is a clever fraud whose transparent, anti-democracy, anti-freedom rantings reveal a man who will do and say anything to achieve his goal. But it is Moore's right to do so, and that right—even when it is used to deliver so loathsome a message—must be protected. It is ironic to think so many military men and women have died or been maimed to insure Moore and his invidious ilk can deceive their fellow Americans.

Anyone who respects, admires, or takes Michael Moore at his word is a chump who deserves to be deceived and exploited by this self-serving megalomaniac whose only mission is to further enrich himself at the expense of truth and freedom.

Pity for the Pathetic

Let it never be said that Marines never take pity upon those with whom they have disagreements. This chapter demonstrates just how kind I can be to the radical left.

Today was a glorious day to celebrate democracy again. I watched the inauguration from my living room, where an annoying bout of acute bronchitis had marooned me. But it wasn't all fun and games, as I nearly died laughing and coughing and gagging at the same time when the camera swung to the protesters. I may have actually coughed up part of a lung.

The protestors from A.N.S.W.E.R. [1] were along the parade route, holding their little signs and trying to get a chant going. I was embarrassed for the group because nowhere near the 10,000 promised by the fascist organization bothered to show up. An estimated 1,500 is all that dared show their frowning faces. This pathetic turnout was drowned out by the throngs of pro-freedom well wishers celebrating the two newest democratic nations, Iraq and Afghanistan, and how they have followed in America's footsteps.

1. Act Now to Stop War & End Racism

A.N.S.W.E.R. wasn't the only pro-tyranny group to suffer humiliation. The ACLU (founded by Marxist anti-Semite Roger Baldwin) failed miserably to achieve its frantic goal of getting 100,000 schmucks to sign their pedantic "I Refuse To Surrender My Freedom" petition on its website. Human Rights Watch wailed on its website about how evil America is. Barbara Boxer busied herself rereading Orwell's *1984* and stroking the head of her inflatable Ho Chi Minh doll. Howard Dean worked on his scream. John Kerry just sobbed over his map of Cambodia, where he once thought he was.

I get hundreds of e-mails each day from fans and not-quite fans. One was from some poor slob lamenting the events of the day in Washington. He just couldn't grasp the importance of such a day and what it means, so I explained to him that the inauguration is a manifestation of freedom. He's probably still scratching his head over that one. Nor could he possibly understand that I would also have celebrated today had John Kerry been elected. Some concepts are just so complex.

Oh and how the hatred flowed from the leftist media pundits, their venomous barbs falling upon two types of ears: those attached to the heads of the mindless dolts who just don't get it, and those attached to the heads of the realists who have woken up and smelled the cordite. Talking heads on CNN focused on the tiny minority of anti-democracy squawkers yearning for a good riot (but not having a clue how to get one going), whereas FOX News Channel focused on the true meaning of the day, although I know Alan Colmes was near tears. Only a moron couldn't see how CNN was trying its best to make the audience think the streets were awash with anti-American hate mongers. In the end, it was sad to see journalists prostrate themselves before the altar of extremism.

But tomorrow the sun will rise and the people of Iraq,

despite the best efforts of Kerry, Boxer, Kennedy, Dean, Pelosi, and their ilk, will be one step closer to their dream. And here in America, the free will rejoice in the knowledge that even those Americans who loath the idea of free choice will be able to say whatever they wish about the 20th of January, 2005.

The best part, of course, is how the intellectual midgets on the left can't grasp the irony of their ignorance and naïveté.

Denver's Would-Be Tyrannical Trio

Many liberals are extremely intolerant and insist upon being hypocrites all of their adult lives. Some liberals are highly deceptive, too. In this chapter, I reveal a handful of them to you.

Some peddlers of hate who try their best to strip those with whom they disagree of their First Amendment rights get away with their extremism. Others, such as the infamous "Denver Three," as the Denver media has named them, aren't all that bright and are prevented from achieving their nefarious goals. When this happens (when extremism is defeated), liberal media scoundrels put their propaganda machine into high gear in order to spin the incident to the far left. The fuel that powers this machine is lies.

Members of a leftist group called the Denver Progressives (read: intolerance, anti-freedom, pro-tyranny, pro-hate), which is an offshoot of MoveOn.org (the radical organization prone to backfires that was amusingly instrumental in John Kerry losing to George W. Bush in 2004), Karen Bauer, Leslie Weise and Alex Young set out on 21 March 2005 to temporarily strip President Bush and some of his supporters of their First Amendment rights. Their admitted plan was to disrupt a speech the president was set to give at a ticketed gathering in Denver. As do many such pedantic hooligans, the Trio for Tyranny were wearing t-shirts beneath their outer clothing that read "Stop the Lies."

Many liberals screech about how they support the First Amendment and support the free-speech rights of those with whom they disagree. They wail like freshly castrated banshees about the USA Patriot Act being a tool of the right to dismantle the Bill of Rights, even though the vast majority of liberals in Congress voted the Act into law. Yet when someone disagrees with them, they try to hide their true agenda and slip into a meeting in order to strip those with whom they disagree of one of the very rights the leftists claim to be defending.

Now they are mad they were caught, their petty, pedestrian scheme exposed.

And, naturally, the usual anti-freedom suspects in the Denver media (Jim Spencer, Diane Carman, the *Denver Post*'s editorial board, et al) crank up the machine while some of Colorado's most notorious, most intolerant liberal jackals pump the gas. One of the most vile and hateful of this transparent crowd is one Dan Slater, first vice chair of the Colorado Democratic Party.

The "Gunny Bob Show" is very popular for several reasons, one of the most important of which is how I go out of my way to make sure both sides of an issue are presented on my show so that my audience can hear all the arguments and then decide for themselves who's right and who's wrong. Given this tradition, in April 2005 I invited Mr. Slater onto my show to give the Democrats' take on this very issue, among others.

As expected, after his appearance Mr. Slater attempted to deceive his fellow Democrats as to how he got onto my show and what happened during his appearance. What Mr. Slater appears not to have known is that I served as an instructor at a classified Department of Defense school in which, among other skills, I taught my students how to recognize and defend against propaganda.

According to the Colorado Democratic Party's website, Mr. Slater was not invited onto my show but instead elbowed his way on.

This is an outright lie, of course, as Mr. Slater had no idea what my show was going to be on that evening and was invited by me to be a guest. He would not have been on the show had I not invited him.

The article said I am a "self proclaimed 'Independent' . . ."

By saying "self proclaimed Independent," the CDP implied I am really a Republican, when in fact I've never been a member of the Republican Party.

The article said I "attempted to paint Democrats as being violent and radical."

What I really said was some *liberals* (not Democrats) are violent and gave extensive evidence of this, such as the 1,800 liberals arrested at the 2004 Republican National Convention, as opposed to the five conservatives arrested at the 2004 Democratic National Convention.

Mr. Slater then said, "Bob Newman began to imply that the three individuals kicked out of the faux 'town hall meeting' actually infringed on Bush's right to free speech."

The truth is that I implied no such thing, but rather stated clearly that the three anti-First Amendment thugs intended to temporarily strip the president of his First Amendment rights but were prevented from doing so.

Then the article said, "Republicans should be aware that Democrats are going to have their voices heard, even on conservative radio shows."

The above quote implies Dirty Dan somehow strongarmed his way onto the "Gunny Bob Show." The truth, as I said, is that I invited Dan onto the show so that my audience could hear both sides of the argument and make up their own minds.

Finally, the article stated, "Furthermore, Democrats will be giving biased commentary a dose of Democratic reality."

The above statement implies only conservatives offer "biased commentary" and Democrats always offer unbiased opinions. This laughable claim reveals how Mr. Slater thinks all Democrats are morons who aren't intelligent enough to know that biased opinions exist on both sides of the political aisle. I know many Democrats who are much, much smarter than Mr. Slater thinks they are. I have no idea why Mr. Slater feels many if not most of his fellow Democrats are idiots.

Incredibly, the radical left, despite its defeat in 2004, continues to believe that extremism is acceptable and desired by the majority of Americans. To this end, the Democratic Party chose Howard Dean—radicalism's poster boy—to lead the Democratic National Committee. Rather than select a level-headed consensus builder, they chose a wild-eyed screwball who couldn't build an effective consensus between himself and himself. Most Americans do not respect, trust, or admire Howard Dean. Sadly and quite tellingly, the DNC flipped off respected and effective moderate Sen. Joe Lieberman in favor of a kook, a move that is now even more likely to cost the Democrats more seats in 2006 and 2008.

So long as the Democratic Party's leadership remains extraordinarily arrogant, so long as the leadership believes it can deceive its core membership, and so long as hypocrisy, deception and intolerance are demonstrated by the likes of the would-be tyrannical trio, conservatives will continue to gain crucial ground.

At this point there appears to be little hope of rational thought returning to the Democratic Party, which was once known for names like Franklin Delano Roosevelt and John F. Kennedy, but which is now known for names like Howard Dean, Nancy Pelosi, and Robert Byrd.

Good luck with that.

The Fallacy That Is the United Nations

Most machines can be fixed when they break. But if the machine is constructed based upon a faulty design, all the tools and expertise in the world will be of no use.

The ill-fated League of Nations [1] was precisely that because the body was inept, corrupt, and almost wholly without virtue. When it was replaced with the United Nations, grand hopes soon gave way to an ugly reality: the UN was little more than a clone of its predecessor. Today that clone is withering from massive corruption, moral bankruptcy, a total absence of vision, and a deadly lack of a critical will to succeed. Soon, it may die.

The primary problem with the United Nations is that it lacks the ability to deal with an unfortunate fact underpinning its very nature: a conglomerate of nations, each with its own agenda, is unlikely to come together for the good of the whole when parts of that whole are blatantly biased against certain member nations. Throw in the UN's staggering criminality, such as recently demonstrated by the UN's racketeering and fraud within its oil-for-food pro-

1. Founded at the Paris Peace Conference in 1919.

gram in Iraq, in which UN bureaucrats took gargantuan kickbacks from Saddam in the form of sweet, under-the-table oil deals. Now add how the UN quickly cuts and runs as soon as its own incompetence leads to mass casualties (their own), such as when terrorists bombed the UN headquarters in Baghdad.

The result is a dangerous disaster that is somehow still seen by many as a viable body with genuine value.

Perhaps the UN's most obvious shortcoming is how member nations like France can manipulate the Security Council. When the UN was contemplating action in Iraq, it should have been a surprise to no one that France, that bastion of quaking, double-dealing jellyfish with the remarkable penchant for surrender, refused to back up the body's own resolutions. I reported long before the liberation of Iraq that French companies and government officials were in collusion with Saddam, a charge that months later would approach fruition as investigations were launched in France and New York that point to both the highest tiers of French government and the United Nations itself, possibly including French President Jacques Chirac and the UN's own Kofi Annan.

We must also exercise extreme caution when considering the deployment of UN troops as a means of settling an issue. UN troops are largely oafish bunglers infamous for their lack of aggressive fighting spirit, effective training, and professional leadership. I mean, if you were a U.S. soldier in a jam, would you feel good about a UN unit from Bangladesh being your backup?

Little good has ever come from this band of mostly self-serving states, and the prospects are slim that it will ever change for the better. Yes, the idea was a noble one, but malfeasance, prejudice, and a cancerous dereliction of duty has poisoned an already susceptible patient.

Let's pull the plug, bury the body, and get on with the business of sewing democracy in soil that has never seen such a seed.

Hate Down Under

Australia suffers from the same potentially deadly malady America suffers from, that being the highly contagious disease of liberalism, which feeds on cowardice, sloth, naiveté, and ignorance. Hate acts as the disease's vector.

Some citizens of the former penal colony of Australia made it exceptionally clear recently that the hate-America-syndrome has turned into contagion down under.

I was a guest via satellite on SBS's [1] "Insight," of which some Australians have little when it comes to the war on terror. The topic was interrogations and torture.

Throughout the hour-long show, one bright, shining lie shone through: the audience, whom I am told are not representative of most Australians, believed Americans are the evil aggressor in the war on terror and America in general consists of psychotic sadists whose favorite pastime is kidnapping innocent civilians so that all manner of *Papillon*-style [2] torture can be visited upon them.

1. Special Broadcasting Service

2. *Papillion* is Henri Charriere's gripping novel of life in French Guiana's penal system.

Some examples of how these Australians think:

1. An audience member somewhere around 60 bitterly complained that America had killed 100,000 civilians in Iraq. He didn't cite a source or offer any evidence of this ridiculous claim, and I was the only one to challenge him (when I did, the audience fell silent and slack-jawed, stunned that an American would dare question an Australian). Yet he and his fellow Aussie sheep believe that, somehow and with no evidence (such as 100,000 new graves in Iraq filled with the victims of these imaginary American attacks) to support his ludicrous claim, the Allied air forces killed five times the number of German civilians killed in the bombing of Dresden on 14 and 15 February 1945.

2. An audience member stated that the American military was going around Iraq kidnapping innocent civilians and torturing them. She gave no reason why Americans would do such a thing. No audience member challenged her, nor did the show host.

3. Another audience member said Americans were torturing people out of revenge for 9-11, a silly and remarkably ignorant accusation that, again, went unchallenged by anyone in the audience. The host was also unwilling to challenge the claim.

4. When an admitted terrorist with the East Timor resistance was introduced as a guest who had been allegedly tortured by the Indonesian army, the audience cheered him. Whereas it is true that both the resistance and Indonesian army committed atrocities in the war there, not a single Australian in the audience mentioned that

Australia was the only country to recognize the brutal annexation by Indonesia of East Timor after the July 1976 invasion. By Australia's supporting the invasion, the Indonesian annexation was given credence and legitimacy by the Australians, which encouraged the government of Indonesia to massacre even more East Timorese. It was totally lost upon the audience that their nation supported the gruesome suppression of a people, whereas America's liberation of Iraq freed a people.

5. When various members of the audience complained that America had invaded Iraq with false intelligence about weapons of mass destruction, thus rendering the invasion illegal, not a soul in the audience noted aloud that Saddam had slaughtered one million people during his reign; I was the lone voice who pointed this out. Again, shocked silence in the audience that this audacious Yank would have the temerity to speak the truth and question the audience's self-proclaimed interest in the well-being of Iraqis.

What appeared most lost upon the audience and some of the other invited guests was that nearly every one of them lives entirely in the theoretical and philosophical world. They've never seen a terrorist up close and personal or had a friend or family member killed by terrorists, nor are they likely to. Still, in their lazy arrogance and from the comfort of their living rooms, Australian liberals, like American liberals, see not the terrorists as the enemy but those who are willing to fight them.

And were the show to have been watched by terrorists when it aired, they would have nodded and smiled like gargoyles with every vile, hate-filled word from the audience.

Given this, the only apparent hope for Australia is

Prime Minister John Howard, who has the daunting task of somehow preventing his people from again being slaughtered by terrorists as they were in Bali, while they themselves loathe those who would lay down their lives to protect them.

The bashing of democratic ideals in Australia goes beyond television. I recently received an e-mail from Dr. Ayman Shrebati of the Royal Melbourne Institute of Technology (RMIT), who was upset that in a column I revealed Hezbollah's potential plans for attacking inside America with at least 10 cells that are already in the United States. In the subject line of the e-mail, Dr. Shrebati said that Hezbollah was simply resisting U.S. oppression. In his first e-mail to me, he referred to America as the "Zionist States of America!" In another e-mail to me, he said that the U.S. media is "Zionist controlled."

Dr. Shrebati's e-mails demonstrate that it is not only some American and French universities that allow extremists to teach students. One must wonder if such hate-mongering is standard at RMIT. Does Dr. Shrebati indoctrinate his students in anti-Semitic, anti-democracy, pro-Hezbollah thought?

As of this writing, the Australian Federal Police are investigating Dr. Shrebati to determine if he is Australia's version of America's Sami al-Arian, the former University of South Florida professor now convicted of supporting Palestinian Islamic Jihad.

Hezbollah is infamous for its fondness for bombing Israeli buses filled with children and other innocents, which Dr. Shrebati says is Hezbollah's way of fighting American oppression. How Dr. Shrebati believes the butchering of Israeli children is a proper means for Hezbollah to fight against what he perceives to be American oppression remains a mystery. We can only hope that Dr. Shrebati does not follow suit in Australia and place a bomb on a Melbourne bus.

And we can only hope that law-enforcement officers in Australia are keeping a very close eye on all extremists Down Under.

Wes Clark: Egomaniacal General or Ingenious Savior?

I've known a lot of generals in my time, during which I learned to tell fairly quickly which were good guys and which were bad guys. Within two heartbeats of seeing and hearing Wes Clark, I knew he was one of the latter and not to be trusted. Ever.

I've served with many generals, my first in the Fleet Marine Force, then Brigadier General David Twomey, being back in the 1970s. Like everyone else, they had their strong points and weak points. But in the Marine Corps, and I am told by professional soldiers in the U.S. Army as well, the leadership trait of integrity is perhaps most valued. Another important trait—judgment—is often tightly tied in with integrity.

In the *Los Altos Town Crier*, General Hugh Shelton, [1] who was Wes Clark's last boss in the military, said, "I've known Wes for a long time. I will tell you the reason he came out of Europe early had to do with integrity and character issues . . ." This statement by one of the most respected and honorable Army generals in recent times, refers to then Secretary of Defense William Cohen, with President Clinton's required

1. Former chairman of the Joint Chiefs of Staff.

approval, relieving Clark early of his command of U.S. forces in Europe. In other words, Cohen fired him.

Shelton has refused to publicly discuss the exact reasons for Clark's humiliating fall from grace, but speculation generated by other generals suggests it was in part Clark's unacceptable penchant for jumping the chain of command by routinely making contact with President Clinton without going through Shelton and Cohen, his bosses. Such a habit is a catalyst for a potentially embarrassing and dangerous foreign policy faux pas. Was it Clark's notorious arrogance that caused this?

Maybe. That arrogance again surfaced in an interview with the Concord *Monitor*, in which the former NATO commander said that, if elected president, "We are not going to have one of these incidents," referring to another major terrorist strike on American soil.

Clark went on to say, "We could be doing much more right now to prevent another terrorist strike." When hearing such asinine claims, many military personnel wonder why Clark, if he truly believes he is the most brilliant strategist ever to adorn a battlefield, led his men into an extremely bloody ambush in Vietnam. (Clark, who graduated first in his class at West Point, received the Silver Star after that move.) If he can promise America will not suffer a major terrorist strike if he becomes president in 2008 (should he run again), then why was he not able to prevent that ambush as a wannabe military prodigy in Vietnam?

In reality, every seasoned military strategist and tactician schooled in operational art knows there's no such thing as 100 percent security. But that didn't stop Clark from boasting in a cliché-crammed declaration that, if made president, "Nothing is going to hurt this country—not bioweapons, not a nuclear weapon, not a terrorist strike—there is nothing that can hurt us if we stay united and move together and have a vision for moving to the future the right way."

The likes of Caesar, Khan, Napoleon, Patton, MacArthur, Puller, and Giap had better step aside and bow down. Wes Clark, the self-anointed greatest military mind in history and savior of the free world, has landed.

Amnesty International and Human Rights Watch: Where Outrageous Hypocrisy Is Rampant and Americans are Guilty Until Proven Innocent

Amnesty International touts itself as a nonpartisan human-rights organization with no political agenda. Its words and actions tell an entirely different story, one of highly politicized partisanship and far-left chicanery that is extraordinarily anti-American. Amnesty International desperately desires to live in a world where human nature and politics are fundamentally changed so that evil and treachery no longer exist, and war and strife are banned by a futuristic world government. Such fantasies are a clear indicator of delusional thought.

Here is part of a report from CNN's website dated 30 April 2005:

> *Forensic experts are investigating a mass grave thought to contain the remains of as many as 1,500 Kurds killed in the 1980s.*
>
> *The grave, with 18 trenches, is in Samawa, 230 miles (370 kilometers) southeast of Baghdad, along the Euphrates River. Most of Iraq's Kurds live in the north of the country.*
>
> *"We know they're Kurdish victims because of the clothing and artifacts that were found with the bodies,"*

said Gregg Nivala, an attorney with the Department of Justice's Regime Crimes Liaison Office.

Nivala said more than 300 mass graves have been found in Iraq, but investigators have only been able to get to two. It is not clear how many bodies are in any of the other graves.

In the late 1980s, Saddam Hussein's government forcibly removed Kurds from their homes in the country's north in an attempt to resettle their communities with Arabs.

"We believe that more than half of the Iraqi population have someone who is missing in their family," Bakhtiar Amin, outgoing Iraqi Human Rights Minister and a Kurd. About 26 million people live in Iraq.

Investigators working at the grave since early April have recovered the remains of 113 people. With the exception of five, all are women and children.

About 15 percent of the bodies had identification cards.

It is thought that the trenches were dug by the Kurds, who were shot right at the edge of the trenches and buried in them.

More than 300 known mass graves in Iraq, courtesy of Saddam Hussein and his bloodthirsty henchmen. In the cited Samawa mass grave, 108 of the 113 bodies removed to date were those of women and children.

There is, of course, no way of telling at this time how many mass graves there really are in Iraq or how many women and children lie in them.

Curious to see what Amnesty International and Human Rights Watch had to say about this latest find, I went to their respective websites. Imagine my total absence of surprise when I found not so much as a mention on either site. What

I expected to find and did find was a front-page link on the Human Rights Watch website leading to a lengthy article that complained bitterly about the new Iraqi government's desire to try in absentia those mass murderers suspected of carrying out these monstrous deeds who are now fugitives from justice, some of whom are, of course, conducting the horrific terrorist attacks we see daily in Iraq.

On the Amnesty International website, the top-of-the-page article read: *One year after Abu Ghraib, torture continues*. The article claims American soldiers and agents are running torture chambers, presumably on orders from George W. Bush.

Fascinating. Human Rights Watch doesn't utter so much as a peep about the 1,500-body mass grave at Samawa and Amnesty International has charged, tried, and convicted God knows how many U.S. soldiers and government agents with crimes against humanity without a trial, judge, or jury.

No one should be shocked by the actions and words of these hate-filled, anti-freedom organizations. Mired in hypocrisy, their long-standing goal has been to subject America and her allies to as much baseless ridicule as possible, while whenever possible ignoring any and all evidence that freedom is on the march in Asia and the Middle East because of the Bush Doctrine.

How many genocidal regimes have been removed from power and how many democracies have been formed by Amnesty International and Human Rights Watch?

Zero.

Have Amnesty International and Human Rights Watch ever prevented genocide?

Of course not.

How many genocidal regimes have been removed from power by the United States and its allies since October 2001?

Two.

How many mass graves will never exist because the

United States and its allies have put tyrants on notice that they might very well have to face the U.S., British, Australian, Italian, and other democracies' militaries if they slaughtered the innocent?

There's no way of telling, but the number is obviously far more than zero.

And now, no thanks to Amnesty International and Human Rights Watch, the Syrian army has fled Lebanon after 29 years of occupation, elections were recently held in Saudi Arabia, election reforms are planned for Egypt, Libya turned over its entire and quite large weapons of mass destruction program to the United States and Great Britain, and democracy has been born in Afghanistan and Iraq.

The response to these facts from Amnesty International and Human Rights Watch?

America is evil.

For those people who hate America, the next time you are digging a mass grave that you and your family will soon be thrown into after a shot to the back of the head, give Amnesty International and Human Rights Watch a jingle.

I'm sure they'll be right over to save you.

The Mindless Credo of Liberal Hate and Violence

The primary reason our nation is so fragmented today is the grim hate and tendency towards violence the radical left suffers from. I experience it on most of my shows and receive a great many e-mails from those whose hearts are as a black as the ace of spades. The FBI is even looking into some of the e-mail threats from liberals I receive.

Being a conservative radio talk-show host with a show that covers 38 states (and around the world via streaming audio), newspaper columnist, and television terrorism analyst, I get plenty of hate e-mail from the deranged left. I like receiving it, frankly, because the more I get, the more I understand why liberals are what they are and how their skewed, hateful, sometimes racist thought process works. Their e-mails give me insight into their dark world, where elections are stolen, everyone to the right of John Kerry is a fascist, and Karl Rove is Darth Vader's illegitimate son.

I also get into some amusing verbal tiffs on the air. In fact, the "screamers" oftentimes get head-of-the-line privileges on my shows because the anti-freedom ugliness they spew makes for great talk. I expect this from the uneducated, but am troubled when the educated act the same way.

For example, I recently debated Ron Reagan on MSNBC and because his mind was so clogged with vile hatred, he simply could not grasp how American military personnel are very different from terrorists. Nor could he comprehend the difference between torture and discomfort. I felt awful for his late father, a great American who in death is no doubt ashamed of his leftist son who sees America and most Americans as scum.

Some of the better e-mails I post on my shows website. I get a big kick out of the writers who say things like R.T. wrote: "You are nothing but a terrorist yourself. You are a disgusting human being who should have been shot in the head long ago and I hope that somewhere there's a bullet with your name on it."

Yep, that's the tolerant left for you. Anyone who disagrees with them should be killed. Nice. Then again, it is stuff like that which caused me to recently treat myself at Prairie Arms to a new Kimber Pro Carry II .45 Auto with a Crimson Trace laser sight and a Michael Janich-designed Spyderco Yojimbo fighting folder. See, I always try to find the bright side! When the liberals come for me some night, they will get a graphic surprise. Oh, and in the interest of fair play, I am very, very good with the Kimber and have been personally trained by Michael Janich himself with the Yojimbo.

Of course, some disagree with me but at least have a sense of humor, like Mike: "You are a bald, ugly American, dark dress shirt-wearing, Rocky Mountain oyster-scarfing . . . Coors Light-quaffing, US 'Heartland' radio quack/huckster/pseudo-conservative snake oil salesman . . ."

I like Mike.

Ward Churchill has been a wonderful catalyst as well. A bigoted hate monger named Joe has been writing all morning about how he agrees with much of what Churchill says about America. Joe worships those who advocate the violent overthrow of America and the deaths of many, many more innocent Americans. Churchill is his god. He hates the idea of Arabs being free and living in a democratic country like Iraq. I can see him now cuddling up to his inflatable Michael Moore doll and cooing softly.

Shiver.

What is helpful, though, is knowing that the liberals still don't get it. They've put another extremist in charge of the once respected Democratic Party, Howard Dean. Hollywood is furious because America didn't sign on to their radical agenda. Senator and Klan official Robert Byrd and his swimming instructor, Sen. Ted Kennedy, quietly drink themselves into oblivion each night behind the closed doors of their mansions.

Last November, America again rejected the lies, bigotry, racism, and hate that had been splattered upon them by the deranged left. The fact that presidents like FDR, Truman, and Kennedy would have wanted democracy for all does not sit at all well with today's psychotic liberals who detest the very idea of freedom being won by a bunch of Arabs they consider to be subhuman and undeserving of liberty.

And all the while, Hillary plots.

The Cult of Keezjunnahbeh

For someone who has been described by a real Indian as a "skinny white boy," Ward Churchill sure can draw a crowd. His plan to sell books, probably get a movie deal, and dramatically increase his speaking fee is sheer brilliance. I want to thank him for providing me with so many hysterically funny hours on the air.

There's an unusual course of instruction taught in the Department of Defense that instructs high-risk-of-capture personnel (Force Recon Marines, Navy SEALs, Green Berets, Air Force para-rescuemen, other special-operations types, air crews, counterintelligence specialists, etc.) the skills they need to resist enemy interrogation, exploitation, and indoctrination. It's called Survival-Evasion-Resistance-Escape (SERE) School and although it is largely unpleasant for the student, it teaches him skills that can save his life. Some deploying graduates of SERE also undergo the Advanced SERE (ASERE) Course. Three of my 20 years in the Marine Corps were spent as a SERE and Advanced SERE instructor.

One of the myriad things taught in SERE and reinforced in ASERE is how to recognize and defend against indoctrination by a captor. Incredibly, a substantial percentage of well-aware students fall prey to indoctrination techniques in

SERE, even though they were taught about them before being tested. The means can be that subtle, that clever, that insidious. So it is no surprise to see Ward Churchill's students and other sycophants—the cult of Keezjunnahbeh (the "professor's" self-proclaimed Indian name, which itself is an indoctrination tool)—presenting all the usual signs and symptoms of those who have been indoctrinated by a seasoned propagandist.

How can we be upset with Churchill's cult members if they have never been trained in the recognition and defense of indoctrination? We can't, especially when the school they attend encourages its students to advocate the overthrow of the U.S. government and total destruction of America. This institutional bias, underpinned by the university's policy of sanctioning left-wing hatred and violence, is a double whammy for the kids who don't know any better.

Even Churchill's pedantic pettifogger, David Lane, an educated man (if only academically) by anyone's assessment, has fallen prey to his benefactor's ruse. Of course, it helps if one is politically, socially, and possibly genetically predisposed to being influenced by such an otherwise transparent stratagem. He was on my show moments after Churchill's "indoc" session ended. He began by launching into a tirade of how evil I am and how he apparently believes Clear Channel is no more than a cabal of right-wing nut jobs who have well-pressed *Schutzstaffel* [1] duds hanging in our respective closets. Apparently, David is unaware that Clear Channel has some radical left-wing stations featuring such extremist kooks as has-been comic Al Franken and "Hanoi Janeane" Garofalo (apologies to "Hanoi John," "Hanoi Jane," and "Hanoi Hanna").

1. Hitler's personal bodyguard unit.

Churchill's recent taxpayer-subsidized speech at the University of Colorado at Boulder was a study in propaganda delivery and indoctrination reinforcement. As I listened to his presentation live on my show, I was swept back to the many SERE and ASERE courses I helped teach. It was as if I was listening to one of my fellow instructors run an indoctrination session on our students. A smattering of truth mixed with outright lies, half-truths, the altering of history, fiery rhetoric, claims of compassion, demands for justice, claims of victimhood, strict audience-interaction control, and repeated insistence that he and the terrorists he supports are right and the evil government is wrong, were applied to his cult, who having no idea what was happening to them, sat there braying like programmed automatons to the beat of a tom-tom. The hapless kids, infatuated and totally devoted to worshiping their god, sat there slack jawed and glassy eyed. They never saw it coming.

I would have graded Churchill with a strong B+ for reinforcing his hold on his young cult, but most adults who have been around were not swayed, nor was it Churchill's goal to sway them. The speech was pure solidification of his control of his worshippers. Well, that and he achieved his secondary mission of selling books and increasing his speaking fee, naturally at taxpayer and student expense. For someone who claims to hate capitalism (Churchill is a longtime student of Karl Marx and claims to be qualified to actually teach college-level Marxism), he sure makes a lot of money and is a bona fide expert in adding zeroes to his multisource income stream. Clever.

I must go now. I hear Churchill's cult out front demanding I appear before them.

Baaaah, baaaah.

The Pathos of the Kerry Deity Syndrome

There's nothing quite like a Boston "Back Bay" blueblood billionaire running for the highest office in our fair land. I suspect Hanoi John will run again for the presidency in 2008, and to that end, hero of the Scotch industry Ted Kennedy has already thrown his considerable heft behind Kerry.

Is John Kerry God?

First, a direct answer: No. Only God is God, and I suspect She doesn't take kindly to pretenders like the socialist senator from Massachusetts. However, there are more and more political analysts and observers who suspect Kerry's infamous arrogance and lifelong belief in what he still considers to be his glorious destiny as the first globalist president of the United States (watch for him again in 2008) are behind some of his outrageous claims, as well as those of John Edwards and others involved in the 2004 Kerry campaign.

No campaign in the history of American politics made claims equal to those made by the Kerry-Edwards duo. For example, during the campaign, John Edwards told a glossy-eyed crowd that if John Kerry was elected, the paralyzed would walk out of their wheelchairs. John Kerry said that had he been president, his tactical and operational expertise, which is apparently vastly superior to every career military man in the Department of Defense combined (even though he has very little military experience), would have resulted in the death or capture of Osama bin Laden. Kerry also said that if he is ever elected, he will win the war on terror, even though every terrorism analyst I am aware of agrees with me that the war on terror will never be won in our lifetimes, i.e., that global asymmetric warfare such as what we are engaged in is the type of war that can't be won, but which will be mitigated for decades. There will never be a VJ Day, [1] never be a ceasefire, never be an armistice, never be a truce, and there will never be a War on Terror Victory Day parade down the concrete canyons of Manhattan. The reason for this is that we are fighting a war against Islamic terrorism, which is almost totally decentralized and is an ideology that exists in varying degrees in many dozens of countries.

Outright lies, the spreading of "urban legends," and the placing of blame on the Bush Administration for everything under the sun were tactics used by the Kerry campaign. Just a handful of examples of these tricks of the trade include Kerry's false claims that (1) we had Osama bin Laden *surrounded* at Tora Bora (a ridiculous idea that has been proved 100 percent false time and again), (2) he had personally met with every member of the United Nations Security Council in 2002 to assess the UN's seriousness in dealing with Saddam (another outright lie; Kerry never did any such thing according to such Security Council members as Mexico, Colombia, and Bulgaria, among others; Kerry made this wild claim in the second presidential debate), (3) George Bush was responsible for a shortage of flu vaccine (a British flu vaccine manufacturer lost its license), and (4) the Bush Administration was responsible for tactical and operational

1. Victory over Japan Day, 15 August 1945.

glitches on the battlefield, such as when some explosives were stolen from an Iraqi munitions depot south of Baghdad. This is like saying the president is responsible for a soldier shooting at but missing a target, a tank falling off a bridge into the Tigris River, or a helicopter crashing because of pilot error.

If Kerry runs again in 2008 and is elected, his Deity Syndrome, refusal to admit the damage his record of anti-defense and anti-intelligence votes in the Senate has caused, and remarkable litany of demonstrable lies (which are not to be confused with simple misstatements, which all politicians make from time to time) will cost America more lives than most of us can imagine.

Perhaps the only positive aspect of a Kerry presidency would be the splendid, embarrassing humor his billionaire wife will bring us. If Teresa can humiliate herself and her husband as many times as she did during her husband's 2004 run, imagine the myriad amusements she will bestow upon us during four years in the White House.

Now that might be an act worth the price of admission.

"Hanoi John" and His Special Friends

The American presidential election of 2008 may very well see Sen. John Kerry once again throw his hat into the ring. Americans should know as much as possible about all candidates.

As I write this column, John Kerry is on a boat in Boston Harbor, in view of the Old North Church where my revolutionary ancestor, church sexton Robert Emerson Newman, hung the lanterns for silversmith Paul Revere. Were Sexton Newman alive today, I suspect he might stroll down to the waterfront and ask "Hanoi John" some difficult questions.

For example, he might ask Kerry if he was proud when he traveled to Ho Chi Minh City (once Saigon) in 1993 to accept the praise of Comrade Do Muoi. [1] The city's War Remnants Museum [2] had asked Kerry to come and bask in the glory of being recognized as a hero of the Socialist Republic of Vietnam. Kerry's photo and bio decorate a wall in that museum. Kerry was clearly honored for being so privileged. We lost 58,000 men in Vietnam. Kerry says many of those men were war criminals.

1. Then General Secretary of the Communist Party of Vietnam.

2. Formerly named the War Crimes Museum.

Kerry has a long history of receiving support from socialists and communists. His 2004 campaign received endorsements from not only the Democratic Socialists of America but Communist Party USA. Oddly, there was no mention of these endorsements on the Kerry campaign's website. I wonder why. Sexton Newman might ask Kerry why he has tried to keep those endorsements quiet.

And if you think those supporters are a tough crowd, they're nothing compared to the violent mob of Kerry supporters who set upon a lone dissenter on the first day of the 2004 Democratic National Convention. That poor soul had the nerve to disagree with the politics of Kerry's wild-eyed henchmen, who surrounded him, brought him to his knees with their threats, and then became so maniacally enraged that the man had to be escorted to safety by the police before the crazed crowd took the next step. Kerry said nothing about this grim incident. My ancestor might ask Kerry why his supporters are so vicious and willing to strip their fellow American of his right to free speech.

Of course, Kerry is also the first choice of such organizations as al Qaeda, Hamas, Hezbollah, and the al Aqsa Martyrs Brigade, who wanted George Bush out of the White House and John Kerry in. Infamous mass murderers like Kim Jung Il of North Korea, Bashar Assad of Syria and the wanton thugs who form Iran's terrorist government, all wanted Kerry to be the next American president. The Kerry camp kept all this very quiet, of course. Sexton Newman might query John Kerry as to why savages like these want him to be president if he runs in 2008.

Robert Emerson Newman was a revolutionary who understood how dangerous men like Kerry can be. As I did with mine more than two centuries later, Sexton Newman put his life on the line to defeat tyranny. It was telling to watch tyrants spanning the globe calling for Kerry to be installed as the most powerful man on the planet.

As someone who first got into the counterterrorism business in the 1970s, I can assure you that terrorists first look for one trait in a leader they hope to target: a lack of resolve. In 2002, Kerry said Saddam Hussein had to be removed from office because he might empower terrorists like they have never been empowered before. In 2003, Kerry said we should have waited for this, that, and the other thing before removing Saddam, such as getting France's permission to do so. And in 2004, Kerry said America was wrong to free Iraq and is wrong to be fighting the war on terror in so aggressive a manner.

Now you know why tyrants and terrorists everywhere wanted John Kerry in the White House in January 2005. He is their dream president. Now those same thugs want to know if he will run again in 2008. But their eyes are also on Hillary Clinton, who is shrewdly moving from the far left to the more tenable center and even the middle right when it comes to what she claims are her views on border and port security and support for the military, the latter from a woman who loathes and despises military personnel but who has become clever enough not to make that known any more, as she did when she was running the White House.

Already Americans and terrorists are looking to 2008 and wondering which leftist the Democrats will select: Kerry or Clinton.

The clock ticks.

Reflections of Heinlein

America has become a nation consisting mostly of self-absorbed centrists who lack the will to comprehend this war we are fighting. They enjoy their comfortable lives and do not believe our nation is in genuine danger. How very wrong they are.

Like Valentine Michael Smith in Robert Heinlein's 1961 masterpiece *Stranger in a Strange Land*, which I read in 1980 while in the North Arabian Sea, I look about me these days and wonder. Not about my upbringing by Martians, mind you, but about what has happened since 9-11 and why it is so difficult for many Americans to understand what has happened—we have gone to war with an enemy in as many as 90 countries who wants to kill every American man, woman, and child on earth, and who is desperately seeking nuclear weapons—and what will happen if we fail in our mission to defeat an enemy whose most dangerous asset is the knowledge that America consists of a fractious, naïve, spoiled people who have no genuine interest in coming to grips with the nature of the beast in which they are engaged in mortal combat.

We are indeed our own worst enemy.

I've used all my psionic powers to predict several dozen

specific events in the war on terror that have come to pass. I've pointed out the hate-America-first tactics of the likes of John Kerry, Michael Moore, Nancy Pelosi, Ted "The Chappaquidick Aquaman" Kennedy, and even the irrelevant and weirdly animated Al Gore and how those tactics are joyfully watched by al Qaeda (these five characters will vote just as Osama wants them to vote this November, of course). I've reported how it was the Clinton administration that first reported twice on the collaboration between al Qaeda and Saddam (Al seemed to have forgotten about that during last week's rant about President Bush lying about an al Qaeda-Saddam link). I've reported on how the United States has a plan we may have to enact to blockade Iranian ports (a possibly necessary act of war that could suddenly and graphically escalate the war on terror). I've revealed how North Korea is using Chinese transportation systems to provide Iran with nuclear technology and equipment. And I've warned that al Qaeda is right here in the United States, hoping to carry out simultaneous mass-casualty attacks on a variety of targets that will make 9-11 look like the good old days (back when we lost a mere 3,000 people in a single day). This latter warning was confirmed by President Bush in October 2005, which silenced those who accused me of false reporting.

Yet John Kerry, whose voting record and statements in Congress point to a man who has no intention whatsoever of helping to aggressively fight the war on terror, (according to polls) barely lost to George W. Bush. And tens of thousands of Americans are raving about the "truth" and "facts" in Michael Moore's masterful propaganda piece, "Fahrenheit 9-11" and how these gullible, easily manipulated fools say it exposes George Bush's link to Osama.

Many Americans no longer have the patience, discipline, or vision to fight a protracted war, and this war on terror, which is global asymmetric warfare the likes of which has never been experienced before, may very well be the golden bullet that fells the great land.

Impossible? Name a country that has endured forever. Name a country in the last 2,000 years that was undefeatable.

Yes, that is quite a short list, given that there are no names on it.

The United Nations: Diplomacy Soprano Style

Although the United States must not withdraw from the United Nations because doing so would surrender our seat and permanent veto power on the Security Council, thus making us vulnerable, America should show this nearly useless body the exit door from our shores. A much more fitting home for the United Nations is Lagos, Baghdad, or Paris.

I recently had dinner with Gen. Richard B. Myers, now the former chairman of the Joint Chiefs of Staff. One of the things we talked about over dinner was the United Nations, which has been stunningly successful of late in providing succor to terrorists and tyrants who have killed many millions. I couldn't help but wonder how many sleepless nights the general has spent in recent years worrying about what the United Nations was going to do—or not going to do—next that would require him to recommend Americans troops being placed in harm's way.

Several months before the liberation of Iraq was initiated, I began reporting extensively on the top-to-bottom corruption of the United Nations, especially in regards to why so many member nations were adamantly opposed to the removal of Saddam Hussein from power. Some of my readers, listeners, and viewers were skeptical when I told them that the level of malignant immorality and malfeasance crippling the UN makes the Sopranos' organized-crime operation look like a mom-and-pop corner store. I insisted that bribery and kickbacks were rife and existed unchecked all the way to the uppermost tiers of the UN, and that there was no way the UN was ever going to side with the dozens of nations who wanted Saddam out, for were the UN to do so, numerous UN officials would suddenly be making a lot less money; in some cases millions less.

Now we find the mainstream media frantically reporting that not only is the UN's now-infamous oil-for-food program saturated with thieves, but that the entire UN is a veritable haven for criminals in a multitude of UN offices, apparently at least up to and including the Office of Internal Oversight Services, which is the internal investigative arm of the UN. In other words, the investigators are now being investigated for widespread corruption involving staggering amounts of money changing hands in all manner of highly illegal schemes.

Kofi Annan, the UN's ineffective, complacent secretary-general, sent a letter to Dileep Nair, the under-secretary general who runs the aforementioned investigative branch, voicing his concern. Annan has also told the world that he will make sure whistle-blowers are not targeted for termination by criminal supervisors, which has been standard procedure under Annan's "leadership." Annan's offices even warned all UN employees that they would be dealt with very harshly if he learned they were cooperating in any way with outside investigators. Here again we see Annan's Soprano-style management technique of threatening anyone who might be considering spilling the UN's pot of fetid beans.

Incredibly, some leftist pundits, foremost among them Walter Cronkite, maintain that the UN is a great, highly effective, and honorable body that has been badly abused by the Bush administration. In one of his columns, Cronkite lavished praise on the UN and implied any problems the UN has are all the fault of George W. Bush. Cronkite somehow thinks the UN willfully and knowingly allowing Pol Pot, the Taliban, al Qaeda, the Hutus, FARC, Robert Mugabe, Yasser Arafat, Saddam Hussein, Iran, Syria, Libya, and many others to butcher millions upon millions of innocent people is just fine and dandy. Despite these facts, Cronkite says the UN is the planet's greatest hope.

Cronkite and his complicit ilk live in a leftist fantasy world, where there are no humans willing to fight for the freedom of those who have never tasted it. Cronkite used to close his CBS news broadcast by saying, "And that's the way it is . . ." In reality, that's the way it clearly isn't.

Let's hope his world never comes to full fruition, for if it ever does, mass graves like those still being unearthed in Iraq will smatter the American landscape.

I, Victim

America has become a nation of caterwauling victims because we have allowed it to do so. It seems sometimes that every American who has had a bit of bad luck immediately demands compensation from his fellow Americans. This victimhood mentality, if left unchecked, will continue to fester until the pus spreads to our vital organs.

Pity me, for I am a victim.

While pitying me, know that, because of my victimhood, which is manifested in my broken neck, mangled back, Patella Femoral Syndrome, and Gulf War Syndrome (all caused by serving for 20 years in the Marine Corps as an infantry unit leader), you must never challenge or disagree with anything I say. Know, too, that my word is gospel, for I have saved lives while putting my own at risk. You must revere me and accept that I have a free pass to say and do anything I wish for the rest of my life regardless of the consequences to others, for I have served in ground combat, leading wild-eyed, bloodthirsty Marines at that. And anyone who dares counter my point of view is unpatriotic and a liar because, again, I served in combat, and service in combat makes me, and those who agree with me, beyond reproach.

What a crock.

Behind me, propped up on a shelf in my library, are my medals and ribbons. There are 16 of them, including the most coveted by Marines: the Combat Action Ribbon. (Yes, the most important one is a ribbon, not a medal.) In a box somewhere in the garage is a thick stack of citations and commendations for various things I did in the Corps, along with many photos of me and my men, some of which show us conducting Marine Corps business in harm's way.

Do you know what it means to have more medals and ribbons than most other Marines? Not a damn thing, that's what it means. What has always been most important to Marines is not their decorations, but (1) whether they were respected by their fellow Marines; (2) whether, if serving in a leadership position, they led well; and (3) when courage was called for, they did what had to be done. You see, in the Corps, demonstrating both moral and physical courage is mandatory and routine.

Real heroes never brag about their bravery or use a citation for bravery for personal gain. Minor nicks, scrapes, bruises, and cuts are never recognized by a Purple Heart, regardless of how they were caused in a combat zone. And real heroes never insinuate that a good deed performed decades earlier means you are a great man who must be trusted and who is supremely capable regardless of the task at hand. This is precisely what John Kerry tried to do in his failed bid for the presidency. Most heroes are disgusted by Kerry's incessant boasting.

But most of all, a real hero never uses his wounds—accidentally self-inflicted via sheer stupidity 15 miles from the nearest combat zone, in the case of Max Cleland—to gain a purchase on the tree of pity. And that's what Mad Max did with his transparent publicity stunt at the Bush ranch during the 2004 campaign.

Heroism and military service do not give one a free pass for the rest of their life. What you do after military service—in words and in deeds—is usually just as important as what you did during that service. This is a maxim any forthright military man will tell you is undeniable.

The keyword being forthright.

Do You See the Light?

Audacious, long-term projects involving military might in far-off lands can easily intimidate those who lack vision. Such is the case with the liberation of Iraq, the results of which we hope spread throughout the Middle East.

James Brown made me smile last night while I watched *The Blues Brothers*. From his groovy pulpit at the Triple Rock Baptist Church in Chicago, the godfather of soul demanded to know if Jake and Elwood Blues could see the light.

Indeed, the soul-singing siblings could see the light. But at first, both brothers denied seeing the light because they didn't want to see it as they stood in the back of the church.

When the world saw the first manifestation of the Bush Doctrine, many believed it to be folly. But soon the people of Afghanistan were free, the Taliban and al Qaeda on the run. Sagacious Democrats knew Afghanistan was trouble for their party, for freedom can be a contagious thing that, if fertilized, could spread through the widespread patch of noxious weeds of hate and racism liberals and leftists had sown across the planet.

This first counterpunch in the war on terror, I began telling my radio audience in the fall of 2001, would soon be chastised by the Bush bashers, whom I insisted did not want the Bush Doctrine to succeed. To the screams of the left, I repeatedly said that, despite their public claims to the contrary, most Democrats did not want America to win the war on terror because that would make conservatives more powerful, thus threatening the liberal machine.

Recently, former Clinton National Security Council member Nancy Soderberg admitted on *The Daily Show*, hosted by Jon Stewart, that the Democratic Party wants the Bush administration's war on terror to fail:

"As a Democrat, you don't want anything nice to happen to the Republicans, and you don't want them to have progress . . . It's scary for Democrats, I have to say . . . Well, there's still Iran and North Korea, don't forget. There's still hope for the rest of us . . . there's always hope that this might not work."

Thanks for confirming my assessment, Nancy.

Iraq next saw the light. With the country barreling toward democracy, the taste of fear is in the mouths of the liberals. The bitterness is intensified by election reform taking place in Saudi Arabia and Egypt after President Bush called for precisely that in his 2005 State of the Union address. Worse, Lebanon erupted in demands of freedom, resulting in Syria hastily withdrawing its troops after 29 years of occupation. And North Korea, now perhaps a nuclear power thanks to Bill Clinton and his mindless dolts, has been contained.

This morning, as always, my e-mail inbox was jammed with words of hatred and anger from liberals decrying the spread of freedom to those the liberals feel are undeserving—brown-skinned people whose primary language is something other than English and who wear strange head dressings and robes. Some of the hate mail was on Ward Churchill and told of how upset the authors were that I was the journalist who first pointed out that many of his words were not protected speech because they appear to have violated U.S. Code Title 18, Sections 2381 (treason; giving aid and comfort to the enemy) and 2385 (advocating the overthrow of the government). The authors are mad that my revelation has spread to many national media outlets and other journalists like Bill O'Reilly, who now echoes my call for Churchill's dismissal on the aforementioned grounds. (I'm glad I could be of service, but why did it take a Marine grunt to point this out?)

Now faces long hidden in the shadows of tyranny are being warmed as they turn upward to see the light, a growing trend at which the liberals will continue to screech and wail. Rubbing salt in the wound are Arab and European nations, even the French, suddenly agreeing that there's something to the Bush Doctrine.

What the liberals fail to realize is that their incessant caterwauling is the sound of freedom to those the liberals would deny it.

Myths and Legends of the Wild-Eyed Left

This book will annoy and anger most liberals because it contains truths and reveals some of the many lies and distortions the left wants desperately for you to believe. I hope the liberals get over it.

One of the more unusual jobs I had while serving in the Marines for 20 years was as a Survival-Evasion-Resistance-Escape (SERE) Instructor at the Navy's SERE School in Maine. Part of this job involved teaching high-risk-of-capture sailors and Marines how to recognize propaganda and defend against it if they are captured and experience attempts by their captors to indoctrinate and exploit them. This job, when added to the experience I garnered while serving in the grunts, Recon, and certain special operations billets, taught me a lot about intelligence and how to tell what's what and what isn't.

Propaganda is the use of bits of truth mixed with a combination of half-truths, lies, innuendo, and misinformation to influence an audience. As a guest panelist on a television show recently, I was pitted against three leftists who all used propaganda to try to influence the audience. Had there been several more of them, it would have almost been even.

Leftist #1, a professor, while railing about America's

imperialist and colonialist agenda to take over the world, said that Saddam was never involved in terrorism.

That's odd, because Saddam protected al Qaeda's massive Ansar al Islam training camp in Iraq, which was used to develop such skills as using ricin as a bio weapon.

For many years, Saddam played host to Abu Nidal of the infamous Abu Nidal Organization, and Abu Abbas of the Palestine Liberation Front. Nidal died in 2002 in Baghdad, and Abbas was captured in April 2003 just west of Baghdad. I suppose they just happened to be in Iraq on vacation all those years.

Saddam publicly admitted to sending huge sums of money on a regular basis into the Palestinian terror machine. Perhaps that money went to buy milk and eggs and not weapons and training for the terrorists.

South of Baghdad in April 2003, Marines engaged a massive terrorist enclave at Salman Pak with 600–700 foreign terrorists from a variety of Islamic countries. Maybe the terrorists were just lost and meant to be in Iran or Syria.

Leftists #1 and #2 (the latter also a professor) said the U.S. armed Saddam in the 1980s. Of all the weapons I saw in use by the Iraqi army, none were American. All were Soviet and French. Then my not-so-learned opponents said the U.S. armed Saddam with bio weapons. In reality, samples of certain biological organisms were sent to Iraqi labs and doctors in the '80s by medical organizations here in the U.S. as a matter of routine. In hindsight, this should have been prevented, but the U.S. labs didn't know any better, and the small shipments were legal and authorized. The U.S. military sent no WMDs to Iraq and wasn't involved in any way.

All three leftists believe we removed Saddam so we could make lots of money on oil. That's strange, because so far we are many billions of dollars in debt from Operation Iraqi Freedom and haven't made, nor are we expected to ever make, dime one from Iraqi oil.

Finally, there's an easy way to tell if a leftist is telling a lie. Watch his lips. If they are moving, he's lying.

Byrd Brain: The Democrats' Own Klansman

One of America's most infamous terrorist groups not only still exists right out in the open in our society, but we have a serving United States senator who was and some suspect may still be a member of that organization.

Note that a murderer or rapist is never called a former murderer or former rapist. That's because once you have committed such a heinous crime, you are properly branded for life with the moniker. Some odors, once attached to one's epidermis, just can't be lost.

Such is the case with the Democrats' own Ku Klux Klansman, Sen. Robert Byrd. Once a Klansman, always a Klansman.

Byrd's own words should have seen to his political demise decades ago, but because he is a Democrat rather than a Republican, liberals look the other way and give this card-carrying racist a pass regardless of how many crosses he burned, how many nooses he tied, and how many African-American heads he forced into those nooses.

What's that, you say? We have no evidence that Byrd actually personally lynched anyone? That might be so. Then again, we also have no evidence that Adolph Hitler personally gassed any Jews. Nor do we have any evidence that Pol Pot personally shot anyone in Cambodia or that Saddam Hussein personally tortured to death any of his enemies.

The revered (by racists) senior senator from West Virginia has had some fascinating things to say about the Klan long after he claims to have resigned from the race- and faith-based domestic terrorist group. For example, in a letter in which he railed about the armed forces being desegregated, Byrd wrote that he would do whatever was necessary to prevent ever having to fight "with a Negro by my side. Rather I should die a thousand times, and see Old Glory trampled in the dirt never to rise again, than to see this beloved land of ours become degraded by race mongrels, a throwback to the blackest specimen from the wilds."

Nice.

Years after he supposedly resigned from the Klan, Byrd took it upon himself to pen a letter to the Imperial Wizard of the Klan, in which he said: "The Klan is needed today as never before and I am anxious to see its rebirth here in West Virginia." But Byrd didn't just want to see the Klan reborn in his home state. No, he went on to say that it was a dream of his to see the Klan again riding through the countryside with torches lit, shotguns booming, and certain necks being stretched in nooses "in every state in the Union."

The appointments of Supreme Court Justices Thurgood Marshall and Clarence Thomas were both angrily opposed by Byrd because of the color of their skin.

Byrd, spewing his racist venom on the floor of the United States Senate, filibustered the 1964 Civil Rights Act.

Mind you that Byrd was no run-of-the-mill Klansman. He was a recruiter for the genocidal organization. Called a "kleagle" in the Klan, he was paid $10 for every wannabe terrorist he could get to sign up.

As a student at the Dynamics of International Terrorism

course at the Special Operations School, we discussed how terrorist groups send members into politics. While learning about domestic terrorism, it was noted that one domestic terrorist had been particularly effective in climbing the rungs of American political power: Sen. Robert Byrd.

So the unanswered questions remain:

How many African-Americans' lynchings did Sen. Robert Byrd participate in?

How many cross burnings?

How many African-Americans' homes did he burn to the ground?

Does he still creep into his lair late at night and retrieve his white robe and hood and lovingly stroke the Klan insignia?

Does he moon over old black-and-white photos of black men hanging from tree limbs, his brother Klansmen surrounding the lifeless body?

When he sees Secretary of State Condi Rice or African-American military personnel performing their duties, or when he sees African-Americans riding on buses with whites or sees them eating at lunch counters with whites or using the toilet beside a white man, does he thrust his head past the rim of a commode and wretch? (The very idea of an African-American general must infuriate and sicken him.)

Many liberals love the idea of a racist terrorist being in the U.S. Senate.

Now why is that?

Author's Note: I drew heavily from my colleague Michelle Malkin's syndicated column (Creators Syndicate, 2001) in gleaning these facts about Senator Byrd. Therefore, she gets much of the credit for this chapter. Michelle's column and books should be required reading for every American. Her guest appearances on my shows are among the most popular with my audiences.

Ward Churchill: Enemy of the State

Many liberals are confused, especially when it comes to Ward Churchill, the reprobate University of Colorado "professor" who claims to be an Indian and who got his job at Boulder because he claimed to be an Indian, but who can't prove it. Here's some information to help the liberals understand the situation.

I suppose I should be flattered.

Ward Churchill, the hate-mongering wannabe Indian "professor" over at the rudderless University of Colorado at Boulder, has given quite a few interviews to various media outlets since this whole thing blew up in the university's already grimy face. I was the journalist who first pointed out on the air that this isn't a First Amendment case but rather a case of possible treason and advocating the overthrow of the United States government. My doing so obviously alarmed Churchill, who sees being interviewed by me as an impassable minefield. I was also the guy who broke the story of Churchill's claimed Vietnam experience not matching his official military service record, which I have in my possession and with which Churchill knows I would destroy him. And I was the one who first published his resumé that he used to get hired at the university, which also doesn't match his public claims of Vietnam service. These facts, my interrogation experience, my hard-ass interview style, and my military background make me persona no wanna talk to when it comes to wacky Ward. Despite repeated requests for an interview, he won't even return my calls. He knows he would stand no chance against me in a fair interview, so he will continue to avoid me like reservation Indians avoid smallpox-infected blankets.

Him heap big clucker.

What astounds me is that so many Americans, including some of our best-known TV news and radio talk-show hosts, have yet to grasp the fact that we are at war. When America is at war, the First Amendment is trimmed back just a tad to protect the existence of the country and therefore our most precious individual right, which is our right to life.

News flash: your freedom of speech is meaningless if you are dead.

According to U.S. Code Title 18, Section 2381, Ward Churchill may have committed treason, which is punishable by death. He also publicly advocates the overthrow of the U.S. government, which is a violation of Section 2385 and is punishable by up to 20 years in prison. These violations are inarguably evident when one reads all of Churchill's publicly released writings since 9-11 and one listens to his rantings since that fateful day. Sadly, I am obviously one of very few journalists who have actually read more than a few highlighted lines in Churchill's "Roosting Chickens" ramblings. I've read every scrap of publicly released writings by Churchill and listened to every sound bite I could find. I trust you can say the same.

Of course, the wild-eyed, screaming left, upon hearing this argument, flails the air and wails that if we charge Churchill with such crimes, we must then charge all Americans who disagree with the war on terror with the same crimes. Such pedestrian counterpoints are ludicrous, of course, because the loyal opposition is to be encouraged so long as it remains the loyal opposition and does not knowingly and willingly lend aid and comfort to the enemy and so long as it does not advocate the overthrow of the government. Simple policy disagreements are precisely that. Statements that blatantly violate the law are not made by the loyal opposition.

So let's forget the plagiarism, academic fraud, insider assistance from powerful admirers at CU who helped him avoid the usual requirements for professorship and tenure, his lack of qualifications to teach the 7th grade (much less college), his bogus Affirmative Action claims, his complete inability to produce scholarly work, his incitement to violence, his admission that he was a bomb-building instructor for a terrorist group, and his indoctrination of our children. Let's go straight for the jugular and charge him with treason and advocating the overthrow of the government.

Churchill is the enemy. Let's treat him as such.

As a refreshing change of pace, responders sending hate e-mail are urged to cite any errors of fact in this chapter.

Newsweek's Isikoff and Barry: A Twosome of Twits

I am never surprised but continually amazed at what some Americans are perfectly willing, even anxious, to do to make an extra buck. Newsweek *did so recently in the name of "journalism."*

Last year, *Newsweek* called and asked if I would be willing to sit for an extended interview with the magazine on guerrilla warfare (someone there had read my book *Guerrillas in the Mist: A Battlefield Guide to Clandestine Warfare*). I had my doubts about *Newsweek* and the little voice in my brain-housing group said, "Don't do it, man. These guys have integrity and ethics issues," but I acquiesced as a public service. The article was published—complete with mistakes made by the reporter—in the magazine's World Wide Web edition.

That was a mistake. I should have listened to that little voice.

Newsweek's Michael Isikoff and John Barry published a bogus story—now retracted after 17 Muslims were killed in riots caused by the story—in the May 9, 2005, edition of the magazine claiming to have high-level government "sources" that told them a copy of the Qur'an had been tossed into a toilet by interrogators at Guantanamo Bay, Cuba, to elicit a reaction from a Muslim prisoner. After the totally unverified story ran and people began dying, *Newsweek* was forced to admit that these two "journalists" had failed to vet the story and that their so-called "sources" could not or would not verify claims made in the article.

However, despite the deaths, damage to our efforts in the war on terror, and the magazine virtually admitting in writing the story that it had illegally acquired classified intelligence, the leftists who run the rag are, as of today (May 18, 2005), insisting that no one at the magazine will be held responsible for the results of the fatally fraudulent piece.

In other words, *Newsweek*'s executives feel that Isikoff and Barry's jobs are far, far more important than the lives of 17 or so Third World Muslims. And so what if their fake story harmed our efforts to win the war on terror? I mean, after all, American military and intelligence personnel are simply right-wing government lackeys who like to bayonet babies and blow up villages filled with women and children, right? *Newsweek* has made it very clear that harming the Bush Administration, aiding the terrorists by giving them more reasons to hate America, and selling magazines easily outweighs the lives of most people.

Isikoff and Barry claimed that they had "sources" (plural, mind you) who told them about the alleged Qur'an incident and also about a detainee being led around with a "collar and dog leash." Naturally, they didn't name that source, which means either (1) the sources knew they were illegally releasing classified information and *Newsweek* wanted to protect their identities, or (2) there never were any sources, i.e., in an attempt to sell more magazines and get a leg up on *Time*, Isikoff and Barry simply invented the story. I'll let you decide which one to believe.

Newsweek says the article was written in "good faith," which is a ludicrous claim given the facts. This piece was penned with malicious intent, pure and simple.

Freshman-level journalism students are taught to independently verify information before running it as news. Isikoff and Barry refused to do this and knew or should have known what the result would be in the Islamic world. That's the very definition of malice in my book and is plain evidence of a classic absence of ethics among two infamous "journalists."

This brings up the question of the media knowingly and willingly acquiring classified intelligence illegally and then publishing it. The mere act of acquiring it is a felony, of course, and publishing it could easily be taken as treason (aiding the enemy) during time of war, yet we see the media do this with astonishing frequency and the government refuses to arrest those who admit they committed a felony.

Why? Why is it that when a news outlet or "journalist" admits to have knowingly and willingly received classified stolen intelligence, they are not immediately arrested, their computers and files seized, and their offices sealed for the duration of the investigation?

Why has it become chic and trendy in the war on terror to aid the enemy, when during World War II such acts would have been unthinkable to most reporters and would have been dealt with severely had a reporter gone over to the other side?

Self-centered media types, unable to see the big picture, say that committing such felonies is protected under the First Amendment. Funny, but I've read the First Amendment hundreds of times and nowhere in it does it say that.

So which is more important: the ability of a "journalist" to get people killed by abusing the First Amendment, or winning the war on terror while keeping as many American military and intelligence personnel alive as possible?

The USA Patriot Act and Homeland Security Act should be brought to bear upon media outlets and "journalists" who knowingly and willingly put American military and intelligence personnel in mortal danger by receiving and disseminating classified intelligence. The FBI should be using wiretaps, reading the e-mails of and otherwise monitoring media members who have admitted to or who are suspected of illegally receiving classified intelligence.

I've broken dozens of stories in the war on terror and made dozens more accurate assessments and predictions in the war on terror. If the FBI wanted to know how I am able to do this, all they would have to do is ask if they can read my e-mails, listen to my phone calls, etc. I would say they certainly could because protecting my country is more important to me than my privacy. This is heresy to the likes of Isikoff and Barry, of course, who would pale at the suggestion that the survival of America and her citizens is more important than their journalism careers.

A listener e-mailed me and suggested that since the liberal media is all for a federal mandatory waiting period for someone who wants to exercise his or her Second Amendment rights and buy a firearm, perhaps we should have a waiting period before someone would be allowed to exercise their First Amendment rights. After all, it now painfully clear that words can kill just as efficiently as guns can kill.

And the February 2 issue of *Newsweek* published for the magazine's Japanese market had a cover that would have infuriated many Americans. It featured a soiled American flag in a garbage can in an alley. *Newsweek* knowingly and willingly desecrated the American flag in order to sell more magazines. To *Newsweek*, it is graphically clear that the American flag is no more than a rag to be used for whatever purpose suits the magazine's editors and stock holders. One can only assume that the ideals the American flag represents and the men and women who have died for that flag are equally abusable and discardable.

Isikoff and Barry's act killed people. Should or will they be held in some way accountable for their act?

They should, but they likely won't, at least to the degree they should be. In fact, just as Dan Rather recently received a Peabody Award despite his scandalous Rathergate debacle, these two clowns might very well be rewarded for their perilous, deadly acts.

And that's just fine with many liberals.

Nation of Islam: The Hate Group from Hell

If you in any way support the Nation of Islam, you are a racist who bears watching by the Federal Bureau of Investigation. Louis Farrakhan and his band of bigots are a threat to American society and are actively involved in encouraging jihad in America.

I grew up in part in the South, back when southern Florida still had sprawling tracks of undeveloped land where bears, deer, ospreys, panthers, otters, and other creatures could roam for long periods without ever seeing a human. This was in the 1960s and life was good for a kid with a fiberglass fishing rod, Mitchell 300 reel, and a handful of lures.

But all was not well in Broward County and Sunrise Golf Village, the latter now known as the city of Sunrise.

Racial problems were in full swing then. In many parts of Florida, the Ku Klux Klan remained powerful and admired by many whites. There were plenty of areas where blacks didn't go at night, especially in rural towns around and south of Lake Okeechobee, and there were places where whites didn't go, either.

Although racism will always remain in the hearts of some, and although government-sanctioned racism in the form of the misleadingly named Affirmative Action still exists, America's race relations have made vast improvements since 1966. But racism is a resilient disease that can infect at will if the right conditions are met.

Enter one Louis Farrakhan.

The well-heeled leader of the Nation of Islam, Farrakhan is America's most prominent racist and anti-Semite. Alone he is no more than a former calypso singer, but surrounded by his scowling, wannabe gangsters and assisted by fascists like Malik Zulu Shabazz, Farrakhan represents a return to racial division and threatened violence that all Americans should oppose and fight against. The Nation of Islam is to America's African-American community what the Ku Klux Klan and Aryan Nations are to Americans of European descent: a festering boil that, if not lanced and disinfected, will become larger, more painful, and uglier by the day until the pus that is its lifeblood invades the circulatory system and devastates the body.

Bill Clinton has a remarkable penchant for demonstrating extraordinarily bad judgment, but his public, brazenly unrepentant support for one of the most vile, ugly hate groups in America is a new low for the man few thought could stoop any lower. His endorsement of Farrakhan's "Millions More Movement," along with the endorsement of Washington, D.C. Mayor Anthony Williams, is a grim reminder that some American public figures still don't understand that racist hate and anti-Semitism are a threat to us all, not just those of a particular skin color or practitioners of a certain religion.

With an ongoing trail of racist and anti-Semitic slurs and claims to its discredit, the Nation of Islam has audaciously voiced its understanding and support of Islamic terrorism. We can only hope and pray that the FBI has infiltrated this extremely dangerous and growing band of racist, pro-

Islamic-terrorism thugs. While our counterterrorism efforts since 9-11 have been focused largely upon al Qaeda, the fact of the matter is that the Nation of Islam, while fooling some dangerously naive Americans, is a breeding ground for extremists and as such could be being used as a recruiting and training mechanism for Islamic terrorists.

We've seen what domestic terrorists can do, with the destruction of the Murrah Building in Oklahoma City being the most obvious reminder of this. Now a former president and the mayor of our nation's capital are openly supporting what soon might become by far the largest domestic terrorist group in the country.

And it didn't take long for Farrakhan to exploit the victims of Hurricane Katrina. Within days of the storm's demolishing of much of the Gulf Coast, he began spreading the rumor that the government blew up the New Orleans levies to kill blacks. Soon thereafter, a race-baiting self-styled civil-rights activist Spike Lee stated publicly that he agreed with Farrakhan that the levies were intentionally destroyed so that more blacks would die.

Tell me, Hillary, do you also support the Nation of Islam?

Traitor to Country and Corps

Fury is what swept across the Marine Corps when one of our own began insisting that retreat, surrender, and negotiation with the enemy was what the Corps should immediately do in Iraq. John Murtha instantly became a pariah to the Corps, which is hopefully searching for a way to get Murtha's name erased from the Corps' illustrious history.

In a statement that has angered, embarrassed, and humiliated Marines around the globe, one of our own—a retired Marine Corps Reserve colonel—has called for the legendary fighting force to retreat from Iraq and surrender to the terrorist organization that has killed thousands of Americans at home and abroad. He has even called for the United States to enter into negotiations with al Qaeda. This vermin's demand for retreat, surrender, and negotiations with the enemy is so committed to assisting al Qaeda in their efforts in Iraq that he has posted his unspeakable demands on his website in the form of an official statement.

The traitor, Democratic Rep. John P. Murtha, agrees 100 percent with Osama bin Laden and Abu Musab al Zarqawi that the Marine Corps, which is mangling the enemy on a daily basis in Iraq and suffering comparatively light casualties, should lay down its arms, call it quits, and abandon the people they are defending in the fledgling democracy of Iraq.

Furious Marines from wars as far back as World War II are spitting mad at the cowardly colonel, and many want his head on a stake in the middle of the Marine Corps Commandant's lawn. Personally, I would not soil that good earth with so disgusting and despicable a piece of offal.

Encouraging retreat is viewed as aiding the enemy by the Marines and is a violation of Article 104 of the Uniform Code of Military Justice, which is punishable by death. Currently serving Marines, active duty or reserve, who encourage surrender are in violation of Article 100 of the Uniform Code of Military Justice, an offense also punishable by death. Because Murtha is retired, he is virtually assured of not being prosecuted.

However, he will be celebrated by al Qaeda and other terrorists around the world. At this very moment, al Qaeda communications specialists are likely prepping pieces of propaganda using Murtha's traitorous tirade as a tool to recruit fresh killers by showing them that even an American Marine (apologies to Puller) believes his allegedly beloved Corps is so inept in battle that retreat and surrender are the Marines' best option and perhaps should, in fact, be added for the first time to the Leathernecks' vast, quasi-mythical repertoire of operational art and battlefield strategy.

Murtha joins the likes of traitor Clayton Lonetree, the Marine security guard who gave top-secret intelligence to the Soviets, and traitor Robert Garwood, the Marine who went over to the enemy during the Vietnam War and was involved in holding and abusing U.S. prisoners of war in North Vietnam while wearing the uniform of the enemy.

The Marine Corps is famous for its members standing their ground and winning fights against outrageous odds.

Battles with names like the Peking Legation, Belleau Wood, Guadalcanal, Tarawa, Iwo Jima, the Chosin Reservoir, Khe Sanh, and Fallujah decorate the hallowed halls of Corps history. Especially repugnant is how Murtha is insisting upon surrender while the Marines are decimating the enemy en masse.

And Murtha recently implied Joint Chiefs of Staff Chairman Gen. Peter Pace is a liar. Murtha is fortunate General Pace did not demolish him, skin him, and build a hula hoop out of Murtha's spinal column and a kayak out of his rib cage.

Marines should ask Murtha if Chesty Puller would order retreat and surrender before the enemy.

John "The Jellyfish" Murtha should be shunned by all Marines and, if possible, legal steps should be taken to prevent this betrayer from being buried in a national cemetery upon his demise.

PART TWO:

Global Asymmetric Warfare and How to Win the War

"Casualties many, percentage of dead not known. Combat efficiency: we are winning."

—Colonel David M. Shoup USMC, Tarawa,
21 November 1943, in a message to higher headquarters.

"I have only two out of my company and 20 out of some other company. We need support, but it is almost suicide to try to get it here as we are swept by machine gun fire and a constant barrage is on us. I have no one on my left and only a few on my right. I will hold."

—1st Lieutenant Clifton B. Cates USMC, 96th Co.,
Soissons, France, 19 July 1918,
in a message to higher headquarters.

"Thought I heard a rumblin',
Callin' to my name,
Two hundred million guns are loaded,
Satan cries, 'Take aim!'
Better run through the jungle."

—Creedence Clearwater Revival, *Run Through the Jungle*

Hezbollah: The Other Snake in America's Grass

America is a far too forgiving and forgetful nation. Hezbollah began butchering Americans in the early 1980s and we have done nothing about it or the nations that support it. When a terrorist group is ignored, people die. Now, Israel is again having to deal with Hezbollah thanks to the U.N. refusing to do its job and the civilized world refusing to deal with Iran and Syria.

February 4, 2001.

Juan Ortiz, brothers Felipe and Fernando Lopez, Alberto Gonzalez, and Alphonso Montijo made their way across the border and into the United States. Scampering across a dirt road that ran between the cacti and scrub brush just inside America, they were disappointed when the Border Patrol agent materialized in front of them from the lip of an arroyo and told them in Spanish to stop, which they did. The agent then took them into custody. This delay meant they wouldn't be able to make another attempt at *El Norte* until tomorrow, following their release and return to Mexico.

Not far from the agent and the four illegal aliens, Mahmoud Youssef Kourani, 30, of Yater, Lebanon, had also just infiltrated America. No Border Patrol agent intercepted him in his hiding spot: the trunk of a car crossing the border (he paid someone to smuggle him across). Kourani had arrived in Mexico after bribing a Mexican consular official in Beirut with $3,000. Soon after the successful infiltration into the land of the Great Satan, Kourani's brother, head of security in southern Lebanon for Hezbollah, was notified that all was well and the operation devised in Lebanon and Iran was progressing.

Kourani hadn't come to America to set up a falafel stand.

In fact, Kourani had received extensive training in terror tradecraft—counterintelligence, weapons acquisition and employment, target reconnaissance, covers (he would become a carpenter in Dearborn, Michigan, which has a huge Muslim immigrant population), logistics, fund raising—in Lebanon and Iran, with the latter's government funding, training, equipping, and deploying Hezbollah.

Kourani had just become a key member of a Hezbollah cell, joining at least nine other Hezbollah cells in the United States.

But the Federal Bureau of Investigation, an evil and insidious organization according to many members of the American Civil Liberties Union, was far from being asleep at the switch regarding Kourani. In the spring of 2003, assisted by the Bureau of Immigration and Customs Enforcement and the Department of Homeland Security, the good guys grabbed Kourani at his home on Argyle Street in Dearborn. He was arrested for harboring an illegal alien and pleaded guilty, for which he served six months. As he was cooling his heels in a federal clink, the FBI kept digging. They were still digging when Kourani was released and awaiting deportation.

Before he was sent packing, he was again arrested.

In early March 2005, in a plea deal the terrorist pleaded guilty to conspiracy to provide material support to the designated foreign terrorist organization and is scheduled to be sentenced on June 14 to no more than five years in prison, a sentence upon completion of which he will be deported back to Lebanon.

Back to Hezbollah.

The government of the United States made a deal with a known terrorist whose brother is very high-ranking in Hezbollah. That deal reduced his possible sentence from 15 years to a mere five, after which the United States will send him on his merry way to—to what?

To become a goat herder in Lebanon? A cab driver? A fisherman? A carpenter?

Why did the American public ever hear about Mahmoud Youssef Kourani? Why didn't he vanish into an FBI black hole for extensive and eternal interrogation? Imagine the potential treasure trove of intelligence he might have provided had that been his fate.

We'll never know how many American lives might have saved had the "Black Hole Option" been approved.

Before al Qaeda arrived on the scene, Hezbollah had taken far more American lives than any other terrorist group with the exception of Sen. Robert Byrd's Ku Klux Klan. Established in Lebanon in June 1982 [1] by operatives belonging to the governments of Iran (Iran allocates $100 million annually to Hezbollah) and Syria, it was Hezbollah that carried out the attacks on the United States Embassy and its annex in Beirut and the Marine Amphibious Unit located at Beirut International Airport. The results were hundreds of Americans dead. I recall shaking in anger in the fall of 1983 as I stood among 241 dead Marines, sailors, and soldiers as they lay stiff and stark on gurneys in the V Corps morgue in Frankfurt, West Germany. I looked into the lifeless eyes of a friend of mine. He still kids with me from time to time in my nightmares.

Mahmoud Youssef Kourani was 12 years old when a Hezbollah member drove a massive truck bomb into the Marines' building. I wonder if he dreamed even then of killing Americans.

Now Hezbollah is here and here in force. Their mission is twofold: (1) conduct fund-raising operations, and (2) be prepared to wage *jihad* ("holy war") in America should America go to war in any fashion with Iran.

If a nation that has sworn itself to the destruction of America, which has already killed hundreds of Americans in terrorist attacks, is sending terrorists into America, why are we not bombing them into oblivion? Such acts are literally acts of war. How many more Americans must die on Iran's orders before we hold them graphically responsible?

Why are we and Europe negotiating with the most deadly terrorist state in existence?

Shortly after 9-11, President Bush promised to seek out and destroy our enemies wherever we found them.

Well, Mr. President, we know precisely where they are in this case.

Hezbollah cells have for years been compiling "target folders" [2] in the United States for possible attack in case America comes to blows with Iran, which is a very distinct possibility, some would say probability, given Iran's nuclear weapons development program (now buried almost entirely deep underground in hardened facilities designed to be resistant to ground-penetrating "smart" munitions).

In an excellent *Washington Times* editorial dated May 20, 2005, the paper pointed out that "Outside of metropolitan Detroit, last month's arrest of Nemr Ali Rahal, a 41-year-old businessman, at his Dearborn home on charges of smuggling funds to Hezbollah, went largely unreported by the news media around the United States. But the story deserves our attention. In Mr. Rahal's house, agents found a videotape of a Hezbollah rally he attended in Lebanon three years ago. The FBI said it found $600 worth of change in buckets in the Rahal home, and that he said the money was meant to go to "orphans"—the children of suicide bombers. Mr. Rahal has been charged with stealing more than $400,000 by means of credit-card fraud. When Mr. Rahal returned Feb. 9 from a trip to Canada, Customs agents found traces of explosives on his passport."

The immigrant (legal or otherwise) Muslim communities of America are the perfect locale for Hezbollah to raise funds and recruit and from which to base their reconnaissance operations for any coming jihad. But otherwise dormant jihadists are also living and working and planning and waiting outside of Muslim communities in middle-class and upscale neighborhoods consisting mostly of white Christians.

If the FBI isn't attempting to infiltrate these communities with undercover agents, which they should be doing, we will lose far more people in any jihad that erupts in America than we should have.

Meanwhile, the ACLU says law enforcement should not attempt to infiltrate Muslim communities because profiling is evil, Handgun Control doesn't want you to have the right to immediately buy a firearm to defend yourself if jihad returns to the United States en masse, and Amnesty International and Human Rights Watch are worried that an American interrogator might talk mean to a captured terrorist.

I trust you are prepared.

1. "The origins of Hezbollah date back to June 1982, when Syria decided to permit the Shi'ite Islamist revolutionary government in Iran to dispatch around 1,000 Pasdaran (members of the Revolutionary Guards) to the Beqaa Valley of eastern Lebanon, an area occupied by Syrian forces. Syria had previously refused to permit the clerical regime in Tehran to directly involve itself in Lebanese affairs, but the Israeli invasion of Lebanon earlier that month and the cordial reception accorded to the Israelis by Shi'ites in the South convinced Syrian leaders that Iranian involvement could

serve to block Israeli influence in the country. An added factor was Iran's supply of oil to the Syrians at greatly reduced prices.

"The Iranian delegation, consisting of both military and religious instructors, recruited a number of young, militant Lebanese clerics affiliated with the Lebanese branch of Al-Da'wa, a radical Iraqi Shi'ite fundamentalist group, and Islamic Amal, a breakaway faction of the Amal movement, which had become more secularized under the leadership of Nabih Berri.

"Most of the radical clerics who formed the nucleus of Hezbollah's leadership had been educated in the Shi'ite seminaries of southern Iraq, particularly Najaf, where Iranian Supreme Leader Ayatollah Khomeini and other ideologues in Iran spent many years in exile. As a result of these ties, they embraced Khomeini's concept of the just jurisconsult (*al-wali al-faqih*), the ideological basis for clerical rule, enshrined in Iran's 1979 constitution. In a 1985 manifesto, the leadership of Hezbollah pledged loyalty to Khomeini and to the goal of establishing an Islamic state in Lebanon."

Source: "Hezbollah: Between Tehran and Damascus" by Gary C. Gambill and Ziad K. Abdelnour, *Middle East Intelligence Bulletin*, Vol. 4, No. 2, February 2002.

2. Target reconnaissance data.

The Many Minefields of Global Asymmetric Warfare

Growing up in the 1960s in Massachusetts, Maine, and Florida, we were taught in grade school that the Soviet Union was our enemy and that our enemy was armed to the teeth with atomic bombs. Our teachers in middle school taught us that when World War III came, mushroom clouds caused by those atomic bombs would kill millions. Not a one of those teachers revealed the real future to us: that World War III would be a form of warfare not between nations, but between nations and terrorist factions. The term global asymmetric warfare didn't even exist then.

It may be a common misconception that Marines spend most of their careers at war with bullets flying over the heads at any given moment. In reality, most of a Marine's career is spent training for war, being forward deployed aboard ships offshore of potential trouble spots, attending schools designed to make the Marine a more proficient purveyor of discontent, death, and destruction, and performing other duties.

Ten of my 20 years in the Corps were spent teaching at formal military schools at Camp Lejeune and in Maine and California. I always learned more as an instructor than as a student, because as an instructor you must truly be the expert in what you are teaching. As a student, you must simply master and demonstrate proficiency in the subjects being taught. But I loved being a student, and because I was trained in counterterrorism, special operations, and unconventional warfare, I was fortunate to learn all about the spectrum of conflict [1] and what we might expect in the future.

One school I attended taught the unique skills required to be a guerrilla, form a guerrilla army, and overthrow a foreign government [2] by instigating a revolution (this school, and operating in guerrilla- and terrorist-infested regions of the world, helped lay the foundation for a guerrilla warfare book I wrote, *Guerrillas in the Mist: A Battlefield Guide to Clandestine Warfare*). Another school taught me the intricacies of terrorism. Combined, these courses and operating against guerrillas and terrorists taught me one undeniable lesson: effectively fighting guerrillas and terrorists in global asymmetric warfare [3] is damn difficult and costly, but it can be done. It's just that some very hard lessons are going to be learned along the way. The trick is to not make the same mistake twice.

Back during the grim days of Mutually Assured Destruction (MAD), when we thought World War III would take the shape of global thermonuclear war (the uppermost

1. The range and types of war, from low-intensity conflicts such as small, contained guerrilla uprisings to global thermonuclear war.

2. The Revolutionary Warfare Course at the U.S. Air Force's Special Operations School, Hurlburt Field, Florida.

3. Warfare against unconventional, guerrilla, or terrorist forces that takes place in many countries and regions where there are no proverbial "front lines" and which makes extensive use of extensive special operations in support of conventional forces.

form of war in the spectrum of conflict), only a comparative few of us were equally focused on guerrilla warfare and terrorism. Those of us who were knew that the winner of such a conflict would be the side that adapted most rapidly to the situation, was the most aggressive, brought the war to the enemy's neighborhood, and stayed the proverbial course, even in the face of political treachery and even when an easily manipulated (by the media and certain politicians), short-sighted, quick-to-quit-because-they-saw-some-blood populace made the going tougher for the troops.

At this point, the three biggest threats to our winning the war on terror are (1) ethically corrupt, morally bankrupt, leftist politicians (Kerry, Kennedy, Pelosi, Dean, et al) who will do and say anything for personal and political gain, (2) a large number of naïve Americans who demand instant gratification in the form a quick, painless, largely bloodless wars, and (3) the United Nations, which is infested with treacherous criminals who will stop at nothing to see the United States brought to its knees. The enemy, who lies in many dozens of countries, including our own, is counting on such people to help them achieve their nefarious goal of the destruction of America and deaths of every American man, woman, and child.

So the question becomes: Which side are *you* on?

Seeing Big Benefits in the Big Picture

Marines are taught to always be looking downrange. Why? Because by doing so one can better understand the big picture of the battlefield. He who does not or cannot grasp what the overall mission is, and how smaller missions lead to overall victory, is a threat to mission accomplishment.

The American left cannot grasp this simple concept because they are controlled by their politics, whereas I control my politics.

I received a call from Denver's KUSA TV's Marc Sternfield the other day. Marc is a producer there and asked if I would be a panelist on an upcoming KUSA gig about the liberation of Iraq. I had to smile at the way Marc soft-sold this obvious political firefight, but I could see he had been put up to it, and knowing I would destroy my hapless opponents (whoever the poor sods were), I snatched up the gauntlet.

Marc followed up his request with the names and billets of my soon-to-be victims: the *Denver Post*'s Bruce Finley and a sitting duck and self-proclaimed low-level former naval intelligence officer named Frank Ohrtman, who is a member of a nefarious band of weak-kneed leftists who call themselves the "Coloradoans Against Bush's War on Iraq," a.k.a.

the "Coloradoans Against Freedom for Anyone Except White Americans."

Fresh meat.

This coterie of commie-cuddling cream puffs is tied in with the Rocky Mountain Peace and Justice Center, which is ground zero for a clique of Fantasylanders whose idea of peace in Iraq is a million dead victims of Saddam, the dictator's mass graves smearing the stark Iraqi landscape, and his torture chambers filled with the blood-curdling screams of the doomed. If these two groups had had their way, the courageous coalition that freed the people of Iraq would never have done so and Saddam would still be in power.

Me? I live in the real world, where mass murderers should be and sometimes are dealt with via the only means they understand and respect: violence. Whoever said violence is never the answer and war never accomplished anything never opened a history book to read about our Revolutionary War, Civil War, World Wars I and II, the Gulf War, Operation "Enduring Freedom" (the liberation of Afghanistan), and the many other small wars and operations that freed the oppressed.

The truth is, sometimes war works wonders.

Such is the case with the liberation of Iraq. The left refuses to even consider the big picture and the big benefits we hope it will produce. And there's the key: hope! Before our coalition removed Saddam, the people of Iraq who were not supported and protected by Saddam's murderous regime, i.e., the majority of Iraqi citizens, had no hope. No hope of freedom, no hope of bettering their lives, no hope of living in any semblance of safety and security.

That has all changed now, despite the best efforts of the aforementioned anti-Iraqi-freedom groups. According to every poll taken in Iraq since Saddam fell, the vast majority of Iraqis are happy the coalition freed them and want

Saddam to be held accountable for his crimes against humanity. And the fall of Saddam has already begun to reverberate in the region, with Libya's Moammar Gadhafi, by his own admission, throwing in the WMD-and-terrorism towel because he did not want to be next on the coalition's list of killers to be deposed.

Freedom is never free, and those inhabitants of Fantasyland who think it is had better wake up and smell the reality of the situation.

Border Disorder

In September 2005, I briefed certain members of Congress and their staffers on Capitol Hill on homeland security and the war on terror from an immigration-reform standpoint. Their body language told me quite clearly that everyone in the caucus room was paying very close attention to what I was saying and realized my points were undeniable to any rational American.

Two weeks later, I read a poll that said 87 percent of Americans want a wall or fence system along our border with Mexico that prevents the vast majority of would-be illegal aliens from entering the United States. Eighty-seven percent of Americans apparently understand that if we fail to secure our borders, our war-on-terror efforts abroad will be for naught.

The president and Congress, but for a few members of Congress like Rep. Tom Tancredo and Rep. Bob Beauprez, casually ignore this fact and, by doing so, place our nation at great risk.

Whereas President George W. Bush has been doing as good a job as can be expected in the war on terror abroad, I continue to be astounded and mystified as to why he refuses to take the war on terror seriously when it comes to securing our borders. I do not know if he is accepting tremendously dangerous advice from some of his advisors on this, or whether he actually believes that not securing our borders is a good risk to take in return for contributions from companies and industries that want cheap, illegal alien labor.

In April 2005, I spent a few days on the Arizona-Mexico border with the Minuteman Project, members of whom President Bush refers to as "vigilantes." Having seen this operation firsthand, and now knowing some of the Minutemen, I can assure you that these average American men and women—who are from all walks of life and from various backgrounds—are anything but vigilantes, and the president should apologize for using such a slanderous term to describe U.S. citizens who are willing to do what he is not.

And they are doing so with no fuss and no muss, despite the disparaging and totally erroneous comments of our president and despite the best efforts of the thugs sent to the border by the American Civil Liberties Union to harass, threaten, and intimidate the peaceful, law-abiding Minutemen, and despite the leftist, hate-mongering press and yellow "journalists" like FOX News Channel's Alan Colmes.

Let's air this out. President Bush and Congress are knowingly and willingly derelict in their duties when it comes to our border security. The Congress and Bush Administration could, if they so chose, secure our border from illegal alien traffic so that just a trickle of illegal aliens were making it across (no security system is 100 percent). But they refuse to do so because, as politicians, corporations send them a great deal of money to not secure the border. This is, of course, bribery in any other country, but here we call it "contributions."

Among the Minutemen are grandmothers sitting in lawn chairs holding binoculars and cell phones. These grannies and the rest of the Minutemen, when they see what appear to be some illegal aliens crossing the border, simply call the Border Patrol, who show up minutes later, thank the

Minutemen, and take the illegals into custody. The Minutemen do not take anyone into custody themselves. Because these everyday citizens have humiliated the Bush Administration by demonstrating just how porous our border is (an average of 485,000 illegals made it safely into the U.S. every year since President Bush took office), President Bush decided it was wise to retaliate by denigrating the Minutemen, and he did so with *el jefe bandido,* [1] a.k.a. Mexican President Vicente Fox, standing right beside him.

An American president siding with the leader of a country conducting a massive insurgency in America rather than holding him accountable.

An American president ignoring the staggering amounts of narcotics Vicente's government helps cross our border.

An American president who is best pals with the man who is personally ensuring that the Mexican side of the fence stays totally undefended from terrorists looking to gain access to America so that they can kill all the more Americans.

An American president who simply ignores the fact that the vast majority of Americans want him to stop sucking up to Vicente Fox and start getting serious about securing our border, which we know from reams of intelligence that al Qaeda is fully aware is unsecured and intends to exploit, if they haven't already.

What's wrong with this picture? And why aren't the American people vehemently demanding that President Bush stop subordinating himself and America to the leader of one of the most corrupt nations on the planet? Why does President Bush think it just great for the government of Mexico and the Mexican state of Yucatan to publish detailed insurgency manuals for their people to use to infiltrate the United States?

1. Spanish for "the boss outlaw."

The situation is so bad that Border Patrol Local 2544 based in Tucson has publicly called out President Bush on this matter and is supporting the Minuteman Project, whose mission it is to call attention to the problem and demonstrate that the border can be shut down to illegal alien traffic. I interviewed an official Border Patrol spokesman during my time with the Minutemen and he praised them. Here's a statement from Local 2544:

"We want to make it clear because we've had *a lot* of questions about this . . . we have not had one single complaint from a rank-and-file agent in this sector about the Minutemen. Every report we've received indicates these people are very supportive of the rank-and-file agents, they're courteous, many of them are retired firefighters, cops, and other professionals, and they're not causing us any problems whatsoever. Reports of them causing ground sensors to go off are exaggerated because most of those are being set off by the ACLU sneaking around trying to find the Minutemen doing something wrong. The Minutemen have succeeded in shifting the bulk of the illegal alien traffic out of the Naco corridor. If only President Bush were so supportive of the rank-and-file agents. While President Bush hangs out thousands of miles away in the White House, these people are willing to give up their time and energy to actually do something. While President Bush entices millions of illegal aliens to keep coming with his amnesty proposals and his demoralizing statements that he doesn't want Border Patrol agents chasing 'good-hearted people just coming here to take jobs Americans won't do,' the Minutemen are trying to get our laws enforced. The Minutemen have made it very clear that they fully support rank-and-file Border Patrol agents. If only we had such support from the politicians we have to work for (aren't we really supposed to be working for the citizens of this country anyway?)!"

But it gets worse. Not only is the president ignoring and lying about the border situation, he is refusing to change the Border Patrol's policy of immediately returning Mexican illegals to Mexico, who sometimes within minutes are right back across the border. And other-than-Mexicans (OTMs) are quickly processed, handed a piece of paper with their court date on it, and turned loose—in America. That's right. If an OTM doesn't "pop" on a terrorist watch list, they are simply given their court date and set free, inside the United States. Naturally, most are never heard from again. President Bush thinks this absurd and extremely dangerous policy is brilliant and ethical.

Another mysterious facet of this situation is how the president agrees with the Marxist-founded American Civil Liberties Union, which sent its violence-prone thugs to try to intimidate the Minutemen in various ways. The ACLU's goal was to create an incident on the border that the leftist media would then have a field day with. Fortunately, the Minutemen were aware of the ACLU plot and trained to defend against it, which they did with ease.

Many Americans also wonder how the president can sleep at night knowing he and the ACLU both think that rewarding illegal aliens with amnesty is a swell idea. Regardless of what the Bush Administration claims, President Bush's "guest worker" program is an amnesty program for criminals, plain and simple, and if someone—anyone—in the White House would pay attention, they would realize that most Americans do not want to reward criminals and most Americans do want our border secured. They want the border secured because they understand an al Qaeda team smuggling a nuclear weapon across the border is a grim and very real threat. And they understand precisely what the consequences would be if al Qaeda were to do so.

Adding to our border problem is Mara Salvatrucha, or MS-13, the world's most deadly "gang," which can be a misleading term because of its way of making one picture some neighborhood punks loitering on a street corner flashing traditional gang hand signs. MS-13 is much more than that.

MS-13 is an international crime syndicate operational in 38 American states plus Mexico and all Central American countries. This is the most vicious and deadly gang there is. They are not a terrorist organization per se, as they have no religious, socio-political, or other such agendas other than crime, but intelligence indicates they have been in contact with al Qaeda and may have already been hired by al Qaeda to smuggle terrorists and weapons for those terrorists into the United States. MS-13 is the gang that carried out the horrendous AK-47 attack on a Honduran bus in December 2004 that left 28 civilians dead, including six children. In Central America alone there are an estimated 25,000 (very likely many more [2]) members of MS-13, which was formed in the 1990s, first in Los Angeles and then spreading out.

On 10 February 2005, Ever Anibal Rivera Paz, whose MS-13 moniker is "El Culiche" (Spanish for "The Tapeworm"), was arrested in Texas. Paz is (was?) the leader of MS-13 in Honduras and masterminded the Chamalecon bus attack. He had escaped from a Honduran prison on 23 January after being arrested for his role in the slaughter.

In Washington, our point man when it comes to border security and immigration reform is Rep. Tom Tancredo (R-CO). This lone voice in the wilderness has embarked on an admirable crusade to expose the White House and Congress' extraordinary failure to take every possible step in securing

2. In the spring of 2005, I returned to Nicaragua and debriefed a very reliable and well-informed source with direct connections to the president of Nicaragua. He informed me that MS-13 is much larger than the U.S. estimates.

our border and ridding our country of the approximately 16 million (more likely 20 million) illegal aliens, hundreds of thousands of whom have committed felonies and, most disturbingly, an unknown percentage of whom are terrorists. Anyone who believes that there are no terrorists among the 16 million illegals here is an idiot.

The best source of information on our border and immigration problem is Michelle Malkin's *Invasion: How America Still Welcomes Terrorists, Criminals, and Other Foreign Menaces to Our Shores*. Michelle is a syndicated columnist and investigative journalist with few peers in this realm, frankly. Her guest slots on my shows are among the most popular and anticipated because her research and insight into homeland security is as keen as it could be. But I will warn you now that you are going to be very angry after reading Michelle's book.

It is only a matter of time before our open borders are exploited by terrorists who then carry out a major mass-casualty attack. When this happens, and if the investigation finds that the terrorists illegally entered the United States via our border with Mexico or Canada during President Bush's time in office, what will your reaction be?

Homegrown Terrorists: Eco-Terror in the Homeland

Eco-terrorist groups are so decentralized that they are nearly impossible to infiltrate. This makes them especially dangerous. The FBI is fully aware of this annoying fact and continues to try to get spies into groups like ELF and ALF. We can only hope that one day soon, the FBI will be successful.

Ask most Americans what terrorist factions pose some of the most extreme threats to America, and al Qaeda will top the list. A tiny handful might mention Hezbollah or even Hamas, but it is Osama bin Laden's al Qaeda that the vast majority of Americans see as being the worst of the worst, which body-count-wise and globally would be accurate. But two of the most insidious terrorists groups at large in America have nothing to do with Islam, and they are directly supported by an organization that is viewed by millions of Americans as being legitimate.

As the war on terror spread into Iraq, the Philippines, Thailand, Indonesia, Pakistan, Spain, England, the Netherlands, Turkey, and many other countries, with special operations forces from the United States and its allies conducting counterterrorism operations, the majority of which will never be reported on in any detail, America continued to be attacked right here at home. Yet many Americans paid little if any attention, thinking the terrorists weren't much of a threat because they were really just some herbal-tea-sipping bunny- and tree-huggers acting out.

Wrong.

When conducting offensive combat operations, it is always wise to maintain a vigorous, pro-active defense at your patrol base and in rear areas because the enemy will oftentimes attempt to attack you there as a means of reducing your offensive combat power. Knowing this, I began warning in 2003 that the eco-terrorist groups Earth Liberation Front (ELF) and Animal Liberation Front (ALF), assisted financially by the People for the Ethical Treatment of Animals (PETA), would take advantage of most of America's counterterror focus being placed on Islamic terrorist groups to substantially increase the number and scope of their attacks in the homeland. I also reported that the FBI was also fully aware of this and that they were diligently involved in investigating these groups and working cases.

In May 2005, John Lewis, the FBI's deputy assistant director for counterterrorism, testified before a Senate committee [1] that whereas in the past eco-terrorist groups had largely avoided directly targeting human life, their attack patterns were morphing in an alarming way.

"The FBI has observed troubling signs that this is changing. We have seen an escalation in violent rhetoric and tactics," Lewis told the committee. "Attacks are also growing in frequency and size." He testified that eco-terror groups are now the most serious domestic-terror threat in the United States and had eclipsed more well-known domestic terrorist groups, such as the Ku Klux Klan and Aryan Nations.

"There is nothing else going on in this country over the

1. Senate Environment and Public Works Committee.

last several years that is racking up the high number of violent crimes and terrorist actions," Lewis said.

Arson, bombings, threats, intimidation, office takeovers, and letters with razor blades to slice open the person opening them are now favored tactics of the terrorists, who receive large donations from their front organization, PETA, which is supported by pro-eco-terror celebrities, including former "Golden Girls" star Bea Arthur, Sir Paul McCartney, blonde bombshell and porn star Pamela Anderson, and the Beastie Boys musical group.

Thirty-five FBI offices are conducting 150 investigations into 1,200 eco-terror attacks, which have cost $110 million in damage from coast to coast. Nevertheless, PETA, which compared the attacks of 9-11 to eating meat, continues to rake in stunning amounts of money in the form of tax-deductible contributions. [2] PETA admits to financially supporting ALF and ELF, yet for some reason the federal government has not declared them a terrorist group. ALF admits that other organizations it receives support from include the Fund for Animals, New Jersey Animal Rights Alliance, and In Defense of Animals. [3]

On August 26, 2003, President Bush said: "If you harbor a terrorist, if you support a terrorist, if you feed a terrorist, you're just as guilty as the terrorists." One must ask the president why, if this is true, his administration continues to allow PETA to not only operate in the open but donate money to organizations that support FBI-designated terror groups.

Also troubling about the dramatic rise in eco-terrorism in America is how some law-enforcement figures suspect ELF and ALF may be pooling their talents, much like the

2. PETA is a 501 (c)(3).

3. These three groups are also tax-exempt under 501 (c)(3).

Abu Sayyaf Group and Jemaah Islamiya have done in the Philippines.

In 1993, ELF publicly stated that it was sympatico with ALF, a fact pointed out by Carson Carroll, deputy assistant director for field operations at the Bureau of Alcohol, Tobacco, Firearms and Explosives (BATFE) in his testimony before the committee.

"There has been a convergence of agendas," he testified. "The most worrisome trend to law enforcement and private industry alike has been the increase in willingness by these movements to resort to the use of incendiary and explosive devices."

Many terrorism analysts believe it is only a matter of time before ELF and ALF, supported by contributions from PETA, ramp up their operations to the mass-casualty level, a grim threat we might be able to avoid if the government acts now to declare PETA and other organizations that support ALF and ELF to be terrorist groups.

Avoiding Flaming Arrows to the Chest and Head in Indian Country

Reporters trying to upstage their colleagues sometimes get stupid and arrogant at the same time. These two journalists learned the hard way that they, too, are made of flesh and bone.

My father is a retired street cop out of Washington, D.C., and my mother was FBI. Perhaps that is why I have always looked for the facts amid a sea of crap.

In February 1991, I was sitting atop a Marine assault amphibian vehicle (AAV, or "amtrac") after charging through a series of minefields and obstacle belts at the "elbow" where Kuwait and Saudi Arabia join. The air was fairly thick with oil smoke and the smoke from exploded ordnance of all sorts. I was 33 and this was my first experience in mechanized desert warfare, and it was coming on a grand scale.

Below me in the "trac" were more than a dozen Marines from my 60 millimeter mortar section and various grunts from 3rd Platoon, Fox Company, 2nd Battalion, 4th Marines, out of Camp Lejeune, North Carolina. We were maybe two miles into Kuwait. So far no fire from the waiting Iraqis had been directed at us, and we had avoided the tens of thousands of mines in the sand.

Suddenly, several large explosions went off to my left front a few hundred yards away. I recognized the detonations as mortar rounds and knew right away that an Iraqi mortar platoon was attempting to hit us. I stood up to see if I could see them but could not. (If I could see them, I could call in a fire mission with artillery or bring in an air strike by getting a compass bearing and estimated distance from my position.) I sat back down and was reaching down into the bowels of the trac to grab a radio handset in order to tell the company commander we were about to be engaged when I heard artillery rounds going out from our rear. Assuming what I should have assumed, I threw the handset back down into the trac without saying a word.

Maybe 10 minutes later, my unit passed what was left of the Iraqi 120mm mortar unit that had been so foolish. Marine counter-battery radar had picked up the incoming rounds and opened up with 155mm howitzers using the back azimuths of the rounds. The destruction and carnage live with me to this day.

It was beautiful.

The smoke on the battlefield had become very thick after we crossed out of the minefields and obstacle belts. Still atop the trac with my M16 in my lap, the trac's 50-caliber machine gun opened up, the orange tracer rounds zipping ahead of us.

I instinctively brought my rifle up to my shoulder and began sending rounds into the smoke bank ahead of us along the same path the trac's "50" tracers were taking. Looking back, I surely hit nothing but air and sand, but as I heard the crack of enemy rounds whizzing past my head, I knew that I had to be doing what I was doing because I was never going to hit this currently invisible enemy unless I shot at him.

Nevertheless, I had to be atop that trac because I could

not do my job from inside. A young second lieutenant in my unit tried to get me to take cover inside, and I had to explain to him that you can't very well engage the enemy with a rifle from inside the trac if he is directly in front of you because of the way the trac is configured. I also explained to the lad that the enemy was quite a distance off, that we were out of the minefields, and that my risk was very minimal.

And so we come to the unfortunate case of ABC News co-anchor Bob Woodruff and his veteran cameraman Doug Vogt, both grievously wounded by an improvised explosive device, 200 per week of which went off in 2005, making them the most dangerous means of attack upon U.S. and Iraqi forces and causing more than 50 percent of the casualties. This is why U.S. military members do not ride around with their upper torsos sticking out of armored vehicle hatches. Tactically, the situation is 100 percent different from my situation in the Gulf War.

Since no one else will, I will ask the difficult question while hoping Woodruff and Vogt pull through: Had the duo been told while riding in the U.S. Army vehicles not to stick their bodies out of the hatches? After transferring to the Iraqi armored vehicle in the same movement, did they then feel free to ignore the advice of the Americans and try to film and report while standing in the open hatches?

If they did this, they were doing what is called "hotdogging" by the military. Hotdogging is doing anything stupid just for the thrill that you didn't have to do for a tactical reason. I certainly hope that Woodruff and Vogt were not doing this just to get some "Oscar Mike" (on the move) video through Indian country.

But I do have to wonder why no other journalists I am aware of are asking about the details of the attack. Are they afraid someone might get riled? Why hasn't ABC released the specifics of the attack and how Woodruff and Vogt came to be standing in the open hatches of an Iraqi armored vehicle while traveling through extremely hostile country where IEDs are so commonly used? Is ABC trying to cover up a major tactical mistake by the two? I certainly hope not.

In war, there are necessary risks and unnecessary risks. I wonder how many men have died or been wounded in combat for taking unnecessary risks.

Cry, the Other Beloved Country

America faces many threats in the war on terror. Some threats come from abroad, whereas others come from within. Regardless of the motivations of the terrorists who threaten our way of life, they all rely heavily upon unique aspects of our society which they can exploit to achieve their goals.

As a freshman attending Georges Valley High School in the teeming metropolis of Thomaston, Maine, in 1971, I was required to read Alan Paton's celebrated novel *Cry, the Beloved Country*. Published in 1948, I distinctly recall our elderly teacher's passion for Paton's book. She fairly glowed as she spoke of the pain in Stephen Kumalo's heart, and on more than one occasion I saw tears in this woman of letters' eyes as she read Paton's words to the heathens seated before her. I had no way of knowing that one day, far in the future, I too would traipse across Kumalo's country, weapon in hand (although I was hunting game and not man, and with a rifle rather than *umkhonto* [1]), where his Zulu forebears were once the most fearsome people roaming the *veld* of what is now called South Africa.

1. A Zulu spear.

Paton decried the horrors of apartheid, which was an especially terrible form of terrorism. Today, in other countries, terrorism manifests itself in many forms, from the communist (the New Peoples Army in the Philippines, Revolutionary Armed Forces of Colombia, Maoist rebels in Nepal, et al.) and the Islamic (al Qaeda and its offshoots, Islamic Jihad, al Aqsa Martyrs Brigade, Hamas, Fatah, and Hezbollah, to name a handful) to American domestic (the Ku Klux Klan, Aryan Nations, Earth Liberation Front, Animal Liberation Front, and Earth First! for starters). And there are those individuals who terrorize others with mere words and images (as opposed to outright violence) that attempt to achieve a goal using unsubstantiated fear and threats of dire consequences as vehicles, such as the deceptively named American Civil Liberties Union (founded by a rabid Marxist named Roger Baldwin, who was a great admirer of Stalin and lived in the Soviet Union to study under Uncle Joe; go figure) and master propagandist Michael Moore.

If you do your homework, you will find all manner of forms of terrorism running amok on our planet. Complacency, cowardice, personal and institutional corruption, sloth, ignorance, naïveté, and wishful thinking are terrorism's most precious enablers. And in today's world, where purportedly problem-solving agencies such as the United Nations, Human Rights Watch, Amnesty International, and the European Union somehow remain revered by many, terrorists know that the aforementioned enablers course through the veins of these cancer-ridden bodies, weakening them, and thus making them susceptible to infiltration and exploitation.

It is time for America—the Great Land—to once again rise above the pestiferous squalor of global decay and assert itself in the one and only fashion our enemy respects and understands: sudden, graphic violence delivered to the most sensitive of regions on the terrorist body.

Our "allies" who decry such tactics are part of the threat and need to be made to understand that vocalizations against our policy do nothing but assist the enemy, and that such assistance is intolerable. If they refuse to cooperate, they must come to know painful repercussions in the form of economic, diplomatic, legal, and political sanctions.

If we fail to fight this global asymmetric war on all fronts and with all our resources, Kumalo's heartache will, like the suffering being felt daily in so many other countries, overcome us.

And crying won't do us a damn bit of good.

The Korean Conundrum

North Korea has long been a challenge for the United States. Many liberals continue to scream for us to invade and depose Kim. This chapter explains why the war-mongering liberals are wrong.

Standing on a dike separating two rice paddies among many, I looked a few miles to the north knowing that what I was looking at was North Korea and all it represented. Being in that close a proximity to a country we had fought before in a grim war and being quite aware that confrontations with the North Koreans were likely in the future was clarifying, especially with a rifle in my hands. The roar of a brace of F-4 Phantom jets being trailed by an equal number of A-4 Skyhawks, Marines at the controls of all four, drove the point home that the world was a dangerous place.

The year was 1978. I was Corporal Newman then and a member of Battalion Landing Team 3/3.

Arrayed along the dike behind me was my 81mm mortar platoon. The boys were digging in as I was making my way up the mountain in front of me with my radio operator, Lance Corporal Storm. When we reached the military crest of the mountain (just below the summit on the same side as my platoon), Storm and I would set up our observation post and commence our duties as the platoon's forward observer team.

Twenty-seven years have passed. I am in my library reading some "intel" sent to me by a friend regarding satellite imagery from northeastern North Korea. Once again, the inherent problem with intelligence is frustrating us: verification. Some analysts believe the North is really prepping for an underground nuclear warhead test, whereas others believe it is most likely a ruse designed to gain concessions from the United States. My sources are among the very best, and they are in disagreement.

Some liberal American politicians enjoy screeching and beating their bony or blubbery chests about how the Bush Administration, Pentagon, and CIA are all ignoring North Korea. These transparent blowhards are trying to terrify the American public by making them believe Kim Jong-il, North Korea's enigmatic leader and the son of Kim Il-sung, who became ruler of North Korea in 1948, intends to launch nuclear missiles upon the United States.

Is it possible that North Korea would do such a thing?

The short answer is yes, but the short answer leaves out critical facts, which makes such an attack less likely than some would have you believe.

Those same politicians want you to believe Kim is psychotic. He is not. Kim is the sane but indoctrinated, centrist product of his maniacal father. As such, he and his generals know that moments after North Korea initiated a strike upon America, North Korea would cease to exist. Our ballistic missile submarines ("boomers") would decimate Pyongyang and every military facility in the country. Despite this fact, the aforementioned liberal politicians continue to insist that North Korea is far more of a threat than al Qaeda is and far more of a threat to respective regional stability than a genocidal Saddam Hussein was, even though

Saddam started two wars, was supporting various terrorist groups with funds and training, and used chemical weapons on the Kurds. Kim has never started a war, is not genocidal, and seems to have never used a weapon of mass destruction. But still, those same politicians have implied time and again that perhaps the United States should conduct a preemptive strike on North Korea.

The result, these simpletons fail to understand, would be the annihilation of Seoul, Pusan, very possibly Tokyo, and perhaps even a city or two on the Pacific Coast of America. Even if only Seoul were struck with a North Korean artillery counterattack, the death toll from North Korean artillery shells filled with sarin and other nasties would be staggering.

Yes, Seoul is within easy reach of North Korean artillery.

The problem with North Korea lies in nuclear arms proliferation in that Kim has assisted other rogue regimes in their quest for nuclear weapons and the means to deliver them great distances, such as his assisting Iran's terrorist government in developing the Shahab-3 ballistic missile, which is based upon the North Korean No-Dong.

To this end, I was the investigative journalist who broke the *unclassified* story of U.S. fast-attack submarines being posted in the Yellow Sea and Sea of Japan (East Sea) with orders to be prepared to sink any vessel departing a North Korean port that intelligence says might be or is carrying components for another country's weapons of mass destruction program. And yes, I do realize that this policy was likely intentionally leaked to me and other journalists after me so that North Korea would know we intended to deal with such a situation with force. I knew this when I was told it, and I was happy to again serve my country's interests.

At the end of the day, Kim is neither suicidal nor desirous of a cell mate named Saddam.

We must continue to strive to keep North Korea in

check, but to conduct a preemptive strike at this point in the game, as so many liberals would have us do, would be insanity.

Instead, we must stay the course we are on and continue to have China and Russia apply what pressure they can to make sure Kim is fully aware of the stunning consequences of his actions if he misplays his hand.

Darkside Is Inbound

The Corps is a brotherhood like no other. The smallest, most elite service in the Department of Defense and the most feared military force in the history of modern mankind, the Marine Corps admires nothing more than outrageous aggression on the battlefield. When a leader steps to the front and leads from that vantage point while placing himself at or above the same level of risk as the slick-sleeve rifleman, the Marines of that unit become all the more emboldened and tend to go on killing rampages that occasionally end up in history books. Such was the case with my friend and partner in depravity, Bryan P. McCoy, a.k.a. "Darkside."

I couldn't see him. In fact, I didn't even know he existed at the time.

He and his company of Marines were off on my right flank somewhere. As I was clearing a bunker along the 6th Ring Road in al-Jahra on the west side of Kuwait City, he was retrieving a wounded Marine from a precarious situation to the east of my "pos" (position). As I was squinting through the inky oil smoke of a thousand burning oil wells, my rifle slowly roaming back and forth for another target, he was making sure his general stayed alive. As I was searching small buildings for the Iraqi I just saw scamper into one of them, he was doing God knows what.

More than a year later, he and I received orders to sort out a problem unit the Corps had in the 2nd Marine Division. He would be the company commander. I would be his company gunnery sergeant. A seasoned first sergeant would complete the trio of troubleshooters, or professional "fixers."

His name is Bryan P. McCoy. At the time, he was a captain. Now he is a lieutenant colonel and has been selected for promotion to colonel. His tactical call sign is "Darkside," a moniker especially fitting for a killer of his caliber. (His battalion killed horrific numbers of Iraqi soldiers, plus seemingly countless guerrillas and terrorists, while taking very light casualties.)

You know him as the man who ordered the now-famous tearing down of the statue of Saddam Hussein in Firdos Square in Baghdad.

A modest man who has never sought the limelight (it just seems to find him), he is inbound to my "pos" in the Colorado Rockies, having just turned over his battalion (3rd Battalion, 4th Marines) to his replacement, this after his second combat tour as the vaunted battalion's commanding officer in Iraq. He is on his way to a high-level military school back East, his Marines having grudgingly surrendered the

"Darkside" in Iraq. Photo courtesy of John Koopman.

commander they loved, admired, and, in a handful of cases, died for.

In a few days, he will arrive at my home for a night's stay.

I am honored. Having retired from the Corps back in the winter of 1997, my broken neck, mangled back, blown-out knees, and Gulf War Syndrome just too much for me to handle on active duty anymore, I didn't expect Bryan (yes, we are on a first-name basis; an unusual but strangely comfortable arrangement for a commissioned officer and a staff noncommissioned officer) to come by on his journey east. But from the moment we first shook hands and the moment I delivered my first salute to him, we saw eye to eye and could read each other's thoughts from any distance. He was the trigger finger and I was his rifle. So when I got an e-mail from him a few weeks ago saying he was coming, Susan, my wife and also a close friend of Bryan's, was not surprised to hear me yelp at reading that e-mail in my library.

"Darkside" drops for a combat nap in Iraq after days without sleep. Photo by Capt. Bryan Mangan USMC.

When he comes (Susan and I will try to break him in half with powerful bear hugs when he arrives, but he is a stout lad, so there's no chance of any real damage), we will have a fine meal prepared by me in my home (the company gunny always arranges for the unit's meals in the field). We will enjoy expensive cigars and drink very expensive wine and Scotch. I will spoil him rotten for a brief while. He will grin sheepishly.

And then he will shove off, for Darkside's destiny awaits elsewhere, as do the destinies of all Marines, from the Halls of Montezuma to the shores of Tripoli.

The Great Experiment

To be blunt, there are many American politicians on the left side of the aisle that do not want Iraq to become a democracy because of George W. Bush's decision to remove Saddam from power. When anti-freedom extremists like Ted Kennedy, Howard Dean, Nancy Pelosi, Robert Byrd, and their ilk say they hope it all works out, they are lying.

I recently gave a war-on-terror presentation to several dozen executives from one of the largest media companies in the United States. They wanted to know many things, but the multifaceted subject that just kept coming up had to do with (1) whether we were winning the war in Iraq, (2) why I believe we are winning when most of the news reported by the media is negative, and (3) whether democracy truly stands a chance of survival in so fractious a place as Iraq, with its myriad religious and political factions, which are oftentimes graphically exacerbated by cultural, nationalistic, and socioeconomic dynamics. Naturally, they also wanted to know how I was able to make so many specific predictions on occurrences on the war on terror that actually came true, when no other analyst in the media has been able to do so.

First the predictions. It is not that I am some sort of

modern-day crystal-ball gazer. It is just that I am fortunate enough to have spent 20 years in the Marines operating in fields and billets that allowed me to garner considerable knowledge and experience in the realm of terrorism. My well-placed connections in some of the world's foremost intelligence, special operations, law enforcement, and security services feed me topnotch information on a regular basis. And because of my position as the Director of International Security & Counterterrorism Services for The GeoScope Group, I am able to stay directly connected to all aspects of global counterterrorism. It really is that simple.

Yes, we are winning the war on terror. I believe this despite what the likes of Dan Rather, the late Peter Jennings, Walter Cronkite, Aaron Brown (amusingly bitter and angry that FOX News Channel's Greta van Susteren crushed him in the ratings) the *New York Times*, the *Boston Globe*, the *Los Angeles Times*, the *San Francisco Chronicle*, the *Denver Post*, the Democrats, and some at CNN want so desperately for you to believe. I know what is really going on in the war on terror, and I know what is important when it comes to winning battles. While saddening, the death of a single soldier or Marine cannot effect the war on terror. The leftist media wants you to believe it can, which is one of the reasons why they tell you every time a soldier or Marine dies. The leftist media also tries very hard not to tell you little tidbits like a certain battle in Iraq that resulted in one Marine killed and 150–175 terrorists killed.

This is not to say we are not going to take it hard on the chin from time to time. We are. But wars are won by combatants who get back up each time they are knocked down, which is precisely what we have done and what we will continue to do so long as a leftist pretending to be a centrist isn't elected. Nor are wars won by combatants who are gullible enough to believe what they are told by a media with an agenda, which in this case is the hobbling of the Bush Administration.

Democracy does stand a chance of survival in Iraq. However, the great experiment we are trying to carry out could easily be wrecked by a once honorable party that has been hijacked by hateful extremists like Kerry, Kennedy, Pelosi, and Dean.

Helping the terrorists even more is how the Democratic Party is being ably assisted by the French, Germans, Russians, and Chinese, among others. If they succeed in destroying the experiment before it has a chance to come to fruition, our strategic losses will be incalculable for decades. If this happens, we will have lost a key battle in the war on terror, an event we can sorely afford.

On Armchair Generals, Blogosphere Strategists, and Barroom Tacticians

One must be very careful gathering intelligence, whether one is a formal collector or an informal collector. Your television is accosted daily with self-proclaimed "experts" in the fields of terrorism, security, and related genres. Many are frauds and pretenders, with only a comparative few being the genuine article.

One of my greatest joys and most notable annoyances is listening to and frequently (almost daily) talking with armchair generals, blogosphere strategists, and barroom tacticians. I love 'em all. In fact, one fellow, a "military analyst" for a cable news channel who, according to his bio, has never served a day in the military (he is a "think-tank rat" at something called the Lexington Institute), made such an asinine assessment of how a certain army division was going to deploy into Afghanistan (he said the unit would attack via parachute, even though the division is not an airborne division), that I found gainful employment in the media because I wanted to counter his downright stupid prediction and the bogus analyses of his brother imbeciles. So I suppose I owe that buffoon.

Another guy on a cable network has a bio that says he is some sort of secret squirrel and implies he can't say exactly what he did to whom and where he did it to them because, of course, he would then have to kill you, lop off your head, download your memory into a Cray T3E supercomputer, sink that computer to the bottom of the Cayman Trench, and post a brace of Ohio-class ballistic missile submarines ("boomers"), each with a platoon of Navy SEALs, over it for all of eternity. He speaks only in the most vague generalities, which to me means he is bluffing but has developed a good routine that some folks buy. I have called all my SpecOps and counterterrorism buddies with whom I served from the 1970s until November of 1996, and not a single one has heard of this man as someone who is a real operator, nor do they know anyone who has heard of him. Of course, that's the beauty of having a James Bond-type bio (real or imagined): you can say no one has ever heard of you because you were such a good spook. Diabolical! How do I know this guy rides around in his car listening to CDs of "Peter Gunn" and "Secret Agent Man."

After the October 2005 earthquake in Pakistan, a seen-far-too-often self-proclaimed terrorism expert who haunts the cable news channels like a pernicious specter and who is involved with something called The Investigative Project, stated on live television that the U.S. military had no one available to look for bin Laden because everyone was helping out with the earthquake. This clown has absolutely no clue and was 100 percent wrong in his idiotic claim. At the very moment he made the claim, CIA Special Activities Division personnel, Navy SEALs, and Army Green Berets were deep in the Afghanistan boonies hunting for Osama. The next time you see this man's giant head and narrow shoulders on your television screen, I urge you to seek information elsewhere.

But my favorite is a scrawny, self-proclaimed former Green Beret (U.S. Army Special Forces) who is known to those of us who really did serve in special operations as the "pencil neck." Sometimes his bio says he is a former Green Beret. Sometimes it says he is a retired Green Beret. Every one of my SpecOps pals, which includes Marines, SEALs, and Green Berets, and all of whom are card-carrying killers, want to choke this little weasel.

Certainly there are a handful of outstanding analysts on television who really are connected and who really do know of what they speak. The very best terrorism analyst is FOX News Channel's Mansoor Ijaz. When he speaks, savvy operators shut the hell up and listen. My friend, retired Army Colonel David Hunt, is very good, too.

So what's my point? I suggest everyone take with a grain of salt the divagations of the media's myriad military and terrorism analysts unless that person's credentials can be verified. This includes some of the generals you see. For example, a general who served in the Air Force as a pilot and a Navy captain who drove ships are frequently consulted on matters of special operations, counterterrorism, and guerrilla warfare, even though they have no real-world experience whatsoever in these realms. This would be like me chiming in on how to paint a cubism masterpiece because I read some books about the topic (Picasso, Braque, and Cezanne I am not). Book smarts are fine but shallow without having been there and done that.

Glory Road: Iraq's Day of Decision

Democracy is seldom easily established in volatile parts of the world where the very concept of freedom is foreign. It is been a very difficult and bloody endeavor to create a democratic Iraq, but progress is being made despite horrific terrorist attacks there that have killed many thousands of Iraqi citizens. Sadly, while Iraqis gleefully head to the polls to cast their vote, American Democrats cringe at seeing freedom take hold in a land of brown-skinned Arabs.

I was driving in my truck when the news of the fall of the Soviet Union reached me via my vehicle's radio. My jaw, like so many others, dropped open and stayed there for a while. Few saw that coming.

Back in the 1970s and '80s, the idea of democracy coming to Mother Russia and bloody places like Nicaragua, Honduras, Guatemala, Panama, Chile, Argentina, South Africa, and other backwaters of tyranny and despotism, was a ludicrous concept to many Americans on the screaming, wild-eyed left. Yet today, assorted forms of democracy are living and breathing there.

No one should be surprised that the likes of Barbara Boxer, Nancy Pelosi, Diane Feinstein, Howard Dean, Jesse Jackson, John Kerry, and Ted Kennedy want democracy to fail in Iraq. These hateful radicals are much more interested in solidifying their purchase on the tree of divisiveness by seeing President Bush's Iraq policy collapse than they are in seeing a bunch of Arabs acquire true freedom for the first time in Iraq's painful history. When these professional, unrepentant hate mongers say they are pro-democracy and pro-freedom for Iraqis, they are lying, for if democracy and freedom take hold in Iraq, President Bush wins and the leftists lose.

The turnout for Iraq's election was larger than the naysayers had hoped and estimated, and we saw more Sunnis voting than what the complicit media insists we would see. There was violence, of course, which is typical of burgeoning democracies in the Third World. But the election came off and for the first time in the history of the Arab world, democracy has been born. Naturally, this doesn't sit well with the dictators and tyrants of the region, such as those in Saudi Arabia, Iran, and Syria, because they know history tells of democracy spreading like a nasty rash. That's why countries such as the aforementioned not only have no genuine interest in seeing a free Iraq but are actually doing whatever they can get away with to foment terrorism there. Even Jordan's supposedly enlightened and educated king is predicting disaster in Iraq if freedom takes hold. Funny how Kennedy, Kerry, and their cowardly click say the same thing.

Did the elections guarantee Iraq will remain a democracy? Of course not. No country is guaranteed democracy forever, as forms of government come and go, at least according to the history books. But there is hope, even though hope is a concept that makes the Boxer brigade cringe and fret.

And we must also consider our own history. Our birth was a gruesome mess, with battlefields far and wide scattered with the bodies of new Americans. But we believed and the dream came to pass. As previously noted, Robert Emerson Newman, my ancestor and the sexton of the Old

North Church in Boston, was in cahoots with a local silversmith one evening during what would become known as the Revolutionary War. When he hung two lanterns in the church steeple, he knew full well that there would be a price to pay for his actions. But he did it anyway.

The Iraqis know, too, that there will be hell to pay in establishing democracy there. And despite the most fervent hopes for failure of Pelosi and party, the Iraqis went to the polls and made history, just like the democracies before them.

When Idiots Run Amok

Soldiers from the rank of brigadier general down to private first class have been held accountable for their unprofessional actions at Abu Ghraib. Fortunately, most Army units do not have discipline and leadership problems of this sort, but when one does, it has an uncanny way of blowing up.

I once had an idiot in my unit for whom I was responsible. I'll call him Private Schmuck from Moronica, Texas. This guy was not dragging a full seabag, and everyone in the unit knew it. He was a loose cannon who would careen about the deck on a regular basis unless I constantly kept an eye on him, i.e., led him with direct, personal leadership techniques on a daily basis. His NCOs had to do the same.

Guess what? We kept Private Schmuck out of serious trouble because of the personalized leadership techniques we visited upon him throughout each day. And this was in the middle of a war.

When I first saw the images of the idiot soldiers at Abu Ghraib, I knew instantly that this was a cascade leadership failure. Then I heard how now-disgraced Army Brigadier General Janis Karpinski claimed she knew nothing about the goings-on in her prison and heard her say that she wasn't allowed in parts of the very prison she was running. I quickly identified her as being near or at the top of the culpable list. Imagine that. A flag-grade officer claiming she shouldn't be held responsible because she had no idea what her soldiers were doing and because her soldiers wouldn't let her into parts of a building of which she was in charge.

In the history of the U.S. Army, Karpinski will go down as an embarrassing failure who never should have been in the military. The very idea of a general—any officer for that matter—claiming a screw-up wasn't her fault because she didn't have control of her soldiers, and claiming lower-ranking soldiers wouldn't let her into a facility she was supposed to be running, is ludicrous. She got off light, too, with only a reprimand and termination of her bogus career.

On the other end of the spectrum, we can't just hold the lower-ranking idiots accountable. The investigation should go after everyone who was in on this deal, between the lowest PFC (perhaps this is PFC Lynndie England, a real class act) and Karpinski. Sadly, I suspect that many of those criminally involved in that chain of command will get away, as soldiers who are poorly led and who are poor leaders themselves usually know how to lie and cover their collective asses.

Unbiased observers know that the asinine stories and accusations being circulated by the likes of Ted "Swim For It, Wench!" Kennedy—that orders for such abuse may have come directly from Don Rumsfeld—are indicative of unethical politicians out to gain political and personal ground. Kennedy is calling for Rumsfeld to resign, when Kennedy and his family used their money and influence to get Kennedy off the hook for the death of a secretary with whom he was having an affair. Cute.

The bottom line is this: A handful of poorly led soldiers and a few civilian contractors with no supervision got way out of control, and now we have a scandal. Lower the boom on those truly responsible and let's move along.

We have a lot of work left to do.

Ain't No Livin' in a Perfect War

War has been described as barely organized chaos. Someone once said that "the plan" never survives contact with the enemy and that the Marine had better be able to rapidly adapt to that fact. Nevertheless, many liberals truly believe that America should be the first country in history to field an army that wages perfect wars. Good luck with that.

It is difficult for me to type at the moment (I'm laughing too hard) because I just watched Alan Colmes of Fox News Channel's "Hannity & Colmes" gleefully holding up a *New York Times* piece that said four Iraqis claimed they saw looting at al Qaqaa after the coalition invaded Iraq. Colmes, his eyes bugging out of his head he was so excited, agreed with the gist of the *Times* piece, which was that, somehow, with thousands upon thousands of coalition forces swarming all around the ammo dump, with hundreds of good-guy military vehicles packing the roads around the facility, and with scores of coalition aircraft buzzing overhead, some bad guys got hold of about 40 tractor-trailer rigs, drove them into the dump right in front of all those soldiers, filled the trucks with 380 metric tons of RDX and HMX explosives (over several days at a minimum if loading by hand) and drove away through all the roadblocks and checkpoints, all without a single soldier saying so much as "Boo."

On the same show, unrepentant radical Phil Donahue said the Iraqi city of Ramadi was in "chaos." Now there's a shocker: chaos in war! How the hell did that happen?

Earlier in the day, I saw John Kerry railing about George Bush not ordering the "troops" to secure that dump. I would have thought Kerry, as a self-proclaimed military expert, would have known that presidents don't issue operations orders to the troops. That's the job of commanders on the battlefield. Then again, maybe Kerry received orders directly from President Johnson (Kerry said Nixon sent him into Cambodia for Christmas 1968, but Nixon wasn't in office yet) to carry out his secret mission into Cambodia in December 1968 (which his men say never happened). And maybe it was Johnson or Nixon who called Kerry on the phone in the Mekong Delta and told him to burn down those villages Kerry said he torched. (Again, no word from Kerry on the number of kids he turned into human torches in those villages. Kerry's men deny burning any villages, but Kerry insists he did so.)

I am continually amused by the rantings of people who have no military experience whatsoever, or whose military experience was limited to an incomplete, single tour of duty. Especially funny are all the Democrats, their shills and surrogates who wail about mistakes being made in combat and that all of those mistakes are George Bush's fault. Any lucid, objective, honest man who has been to war knows that war *is* chaos and mistakes are the most common thing on the battlefield. This has always been a fundamental fact of war. But you would never know that by listening to the maniacal left and the rabid extremists at the *New York Times*, CBS, ABC, the *Los Angeles Times*, the *Boston Globe*, and so on. These dolts think war should be quick, clean, and orderly.

Where they came up with such an idea remains a mystery. Maybe legendary warriors like Bruce Springsteen, Susan Sarandon, Sean Penn, Michael Moore, Al Franken, or Alec Baldwin told them.

But that's the fun of listening to tavern tacticians, couch-borne commanders, think-tank rats, and Green Room commandos. Their naïveté, world-class arrogance, and alarming ignorance lend endless fodder to the likes of me who have extensive military experience. And we appreciate the guffaws.

Lumpia, Pancit, San Miguel, and Tens of Thousands of Terrorists

Few Americans pay attention to what happens in the Philippines. This is a shame, because events in the Philippines oftentimes have an impact on the United States. And very few Americans have any idea just how closely our two nations are linked via the history and interests we share.

"This is going to be fun," Norm said.

My part Aleut pal from Cordova, Alaska, and I were standing halfway across the "Shit River" bridge that, in 1978, joined the Subic Bay Naval Station with the ultimate den of iniquity, Olongapo City, in the Republic of the Philippines. Our eyes were gawking in disbelief at the raucous scene before us that lined Maysaysay Drive, the town's main drag.

This was Sin City, where exotic *Filipinas* and ice-cold San Miguel beer beckoned to young Marines such as ourselves. Olongapo was the Wild, Wild East, where "anything goes" was a laughable understatement and debauchery was served for breakfast.

This was the first time I ventured into a country where terrorism was a genuine threat.

On the island of Luzon where Olongapo is located, the

primary threat in 1978 was the New People's Army (NPA), a deadly Marxist group that was attempting to overthrow the government of Ferdinand Marcos and his shoe-hog wife, Imelda.

The NPA wasn't foolish enough to engage a Marine unit while it was training in the field in places like Zambales Province. Not only would the NPA find the Marines wouldn't take kindly to an attack, but the Philippine Constabulary (PC) officers we always had with us were especially brutal and intolerant of any terrorist foolishness. (The PC was established in 1901 by the U.S. administration. Its reputation for ruthlessness is well deserved.) Mostly the NPA would send people to our campsites at night to attempt to steal some of our weapons. Oftentimes the NPA would tell children from a nearby village to try to steal the weapons, for which the NPA would pay them a small sum.

I was familiar at the time with the communist (mostly around Manila and other urban areas) and socialist (mostly rural) Hukbalahap or "Huk" insurgency, which began in earnest in 1946 and ran till 1954, when it was defeated by a classic counterinsurgency program. The NPA was formed in 1969 in part by absorbing some of the former Huks. I recall wondering if this insurgency stood a chance of growing and becoming a genuine threat to stability (as it was) in the Philippines.

A small PC unit in 1926.

In November 2001, I made my second accurate assessment in what was to happen in the war on terror (the first was that tribal and factional collusion would contribute to the escape of Osama bin Laden at Tora Bora). I said that the United States would immediately commence a major military buildup in the Philippines to destroy the al Qaeda-linked Abu Sayyaf group, which had become a dire threat in the southern Philippines and which was poised to expand its operations north to Manila. Shortly after this prediction, U.S. special operations forces in the form of Green Berets (U.S. Army Special Forces), Navy SEALs (Sea-Air-Land) and Marines began the buildup and counterterrorism program I knew was coming.

As I said, this was my second accurate assessment/prediction in the war on terror, and my fellow Clear Channel (where I had been for about a month) employees began to look at me funny, wondering how this Marine grunt could hit the bull's eye twice out of two shots. It was immediately after this stunt that FOX News Channel called and asked me for the first time to come on and assess some situations for them.

Why no one else beat me to that punch I don't know. It was simply a matter of knowing history and knowing what was going on in the Philippines at that time. Naturally, the media and apparently many Americans thought this was some sort of magic trick, when in reality it was entry-level intelligence analysis.

In 1995, Ramzi Yousef, who was being sought for his major role in the 1993 World Trade Center bombing and who carried an Iraqi passport, was renting an apartment in Ermita when some chemicals being mixed there for use in blowing up eleven commercial jetliners caught fire. A computer found there after the fire revealed the astounding plot.

On 23 March 2004, putting the Yousef intelligence together with a lot more that I was receiving from the Philippines, much of which had to do with the 14 February bombing and subsequent sinking of Superferry 14 in Manila Bay with great loss of life, caused me to issue a warning via The GeoScope Group, for which I am their director of international security and counterterrorism services, that Metro Manila was under an immediate threat of attacks on additional mass transportation and other "soft" targets, and that extreme caution should be used in the Metro Manila area.

Eight days later, the government of the Philippines announced the arrest of four al Qaeda-linked Abu Sayyaf Group terrorists who were about to target mass transportation systems and other "soft" targets in and around Metro Manila.

On 4 May 2004, I warned that the Indonesia-based, al Qaeda-linked Jemaah Islamiya had expanded into the Philippines and was conducting training and planning joint operations with Abu Sayyaf, and that this development substantially increased the danger of attacks there. Two days later, Philippines Defense Secretary Eduardo Ermita confirmed my report.

In the last year, the Philippines has been the scene of many dramas played out by terrorists (communist and Muslim) and security forces there. Terrorist attacks there are very commonplace, and a huge amount of good counterterrorism work has been done by the government of the Philippines and in some cases U.S. assets assisting the Philippines. Yet seldom is any of this mentioned in the American media, primarily because the American media has a shocking dearth of investigative reporters who are qualified to delve into the Philippines situation, nor are there many who are even interested in the Philippines angle, despite my accurate public assessments.

Why the Philippines?

It has to do with the southern Philippines being part of a plan by Muslim extremists to create a Muslim nation out of southern Thailand and parts of Malaysia and Indonesia. The southern Philippines has a large Muslim population and would be part of this nation.

Watch for the Philippines to continue to grow as a key locale in the war on terror. And watch for few if any American journalists to properly cover the story.

A Short Ways Down A Long, Deadly Road

Some wars, like the one in The Mouse That Roared *and the liberation of Grenada in 1983, are mercifully short. Others are terribly long. The war on terror, most Americans seem to have a hard time understanding, falls into the latter category. Unfortunately, we as a nation will never accept this.*

"When are we going to be there?" my sister Ellen queried from the back seat of our VW bus. The year was 1967.

"We'll be there when we get there," came the predictable reply from my father at the wheel, a White Owl cigar jammed in his mouth.

The same whining, impatient question is asked innumerable times daily these days by countless Americans, with the "there" being the day we are victorious in the war on terror so that things can get back to normal.

America's patience today is like that of a five-year-old child and its understanding of this war on terror we are in is at the same level.

As the second tower came down in thunderous dust and dying steel, I stood before my television with clenched fists and a tight jaw knowing that my country would soon embark upon the longest war in its history. I also knew that three of the most important assets to our enemy were America's embarrassing impatience, a government bureaucracy known for its fabled ineptitude, and the many liberal Americans (including politicians) who for a while would claim to want to fight the war on terror with the required aggression but who would soon begin squawking and crying about matters they ought not to squawk and whine about.

I regret to inform you of how right I was.

Three months after 9-11, I was standing in a security line about to board a flight at Denver International Airport. I did not bother to disguise my disgust with the whimpering Americans in line with me who were complaining about the security line. And I was not surprised but nevertheless angered when the two security guards running the screening point beside the plane's door pulled me aside for a last moment search of my carry-on bag.

Why was I angry?

The two fellows right behind me were Arabs in their twenties who quickly boarded the plane.

As the two security personnel went through my bag, one asked for my identification. I handed him my Marine Corps and Clear Channel ID cards.

"I thought that was you, Gunny Bob," the male security guard said. "I listen to you all the time and I've seen you on FOX News Channel."

"Then why did you pull me out of line? You know I am one of the good guys," I asked.

"Sorry Gunny, but the rules say we have to take the first person and the last person in line," came the reply.

"Did you notice that the two guys right behind me were twenty-something Arab males?" I asked.

"Yes, Gunny, but we are not allowed to profile."

"Jesus H. Christ man, does that make sense to you?" I

asked. "You knowingly pull a retired Marine and well-known media personality out of line to see if he is a terrorist and let the two most likely bad guys onto the plane without a secondary search?"

"Sorry, Gunny. We are just doing our jobs. We don't write the rules but we do have to follow them," came the sheepish, apologetic answer.

I boarded the plane and took my aisle seat in row number two, right behind the row where the two Arab males were seated. Around my neck beneath my shirt was hanging a ceramic fighting knife (non-detectable by magnetometers) on a quick-release clip. (There was no way I was going to entrust my life and the lives of about 200 others in the hands of some just-over-minimum-wage flunkies.) If they made a move for the cockpit door during the flight, they'd be deader than Hoffa before they could say *Allahu Akbar* (Arabic for "God is great"). By the time they hit the deck, they'd have more holes in them than an O.J. Simpson alibi. I probably wouldn't even spill my vodka martini.

This incident reinforced in my brain-housing group the knowledge that this war is not only going to a long one, but one where mindless dolts infest every level of the bureaucracy and the incompetent are called "government experts."

I am writing this chapter on 1 May 2005. The television news program on is telling me that a new report says terrorists threats to the American homeland are down 25 to 50%. I shake my head, knowing that many Americans will cheerfully accept that report at face value and believe it is a sign that soon the war on terror will be over and seem like it was only a bad dream.

Reality is much more stark.

At this point, we are only a short ways down a long, deadly road, and although we have lost fewer than 2,000

Americans since the war on terror began, that number is destined to rise dramatically in the coming years.

Whereas it is happily true that we have killed a staggering number of terrorists in Afghanistan, Iraq, Saudi Arabia, Kuwait, Jordan, Uzbekistan, Ukraine, Yemen, Thailand, Israel, the Philippines, Indonesia, Russia and elsewhere since October 2001, the grim fact of the matter is that their deaths are a mere drop in the proverbial bucket.

Yes, there have been some important improvements in port security here and abroad. Yes, the USA Patriot Act is a wonderful tool that has saved untold American lives. Yes, our military is better equipped and trained today to fight the war on terror than it was four years ago. But despite the usually good intentions of President Bush and despite a handful of members of Congress who understand the true scope and nature of the threat and who are willing to fight the war the way it needs to be fought, America remains at unacceptable (to me at least) risk.

Our towns, cities and states assume the terrorists will not strike them because of the target-rich environment that the odds say will keep them safe. Our commercial airports pretend to be secure, but are in fact ridiculously unsecured. Our general aviation airports don't understand or don't care that a business jet in the wrong hands could kill thousands. Our chemical plants are ripe for attacks that would make the World Trade Center attacks look like a fine day. The maritime industry remains riddled with security shortcomings. Our power plants think they are safe. Skyscrapers with underground garages don't have security systems that would prevent a 1993 WTC-style attack. Our rail systems are virtually undefended, even though our trains carry chemicals that could kill shocking numbers in a short while. Our borders are so porous that an al Qaeda team would likely spend several minutes laughing hysterically after they crossed into America from Canada or Mexico. And what school in America is prepared for a Beslan-style assault?

In the first week of May 2005, two reports (one from the Department of Energy and one from the White House's Homeland Security Council) on the state of America's preparedness to deal with the aftermath of a nuclear strike revealed that the United States isn't even close to being prepared to handle such an event, even though we have known for years that terrorists are desperately trying to acquire nuclear weapons for detonation in America. Incompetence, dereliction of duty and an almost total absence of any sense of urgency among the imbecilic bureaucrats and politicians responsible for this unacceptable situation are why the terrorists are likely to one day succeed.

As we take the next step on this perilous journey, if we were to look up from our feet for a moment, we would see that the road ahead is an endless minefield.

Unfortunately, the buffoons, oafs, simpletons and twits we are forced to travel with are playing grab ass and asking when we are going to be there.

Spain's Spineless Surrender to Al Qaeda

Whatever brilliant Spanish strategist who decided, with the backing of the Spanish people, that surrender is the best policy when dealing with terrorists, will one day learn such a strategy is no strategy at all.

Back in the 1970s as a 21-year-old Marine sergeant and forward observer in a "grunt" (infantry) company in the Pacific, I decided one day that I needed more of a challenge than I was getting in the grunts. The obvious solution was to try out for the local reconnaissance, or "Recon," unit, which had a reputation for requiring applicants to pass the most severe physical entrance test in the Corps.

Twelve of us grunts showed up at the "compound" where Alpha Company, 3rd Reconnaissance Battalion, was headquartered. When it was all said and done, after what I can best describe as the most strenuous ordeal I had undergone in the Corps to that date, there were two of us left standing. Hurt, bleeding a little, limping and exhausted, but standing nonetheless. I wasn't really sure how I had done it, but I was now a member of the Corps' fabled Recon, the ultra-elite Leathernecks who formed the Marines' equivalent of the Navy SEALs and Royal Marines Special Boat Squadron (SBS).

Little did I know that my foray into this extreme world

would eventually see me breaking my neck on a parachute jump, conducting clandestine diving operations off submarines, sneaking aboard various ships on "sabotage" training missions, learning the art of "Direct Action" in counterterrorism operations, and other James Bondish stuff. It was like living in a Hollywood action movie.

Later in my career, I would find myself living in a terrorist-infested part of the world and teaching counterterrorism. I suppose it all added up to having a thorough understanding of the myriad dangers, tactics, and strategy in the world of terrorism, and one principle was made clear again and again: if you quit and let the bad guys win, they will be all the more encouraged and kill all the more people.

Spain understands this, of course, but simply does not care. In their recent elections, our fair-weather friends the Spaniards surrendered to the terrorists, and now al Qaeda will increase their attacks on other European nations because they know their tactics have a chance of achieving their goals. Spain allowed a terrorist organization to directly affect the outcome of an election in a free, democratic country for the first time in history. This is indeed an ominous turn of events that will unquestionably result in the graphic deaths of many more free people.

Cowardice is not only despicable but frequently deadly. The French, Germans, and Belgians refuse to fight the terrorists outside of their respective borders, which makes the terrorists stronger and more aggressive. Now Spain has joined this loathsome lot, this covey of cowering cretins, and the cancer they have fostered may very well spread to other nations, which is precisely what Osama bin Laden is hoping for.

Make no mistake about it: more Americans will die now that the cringing people of Spain have shown, like the French, Germans, and Belgians, their true colors, which in this case are all shades of yellow.

The Reality of War and the Tun Tavern Solution

The Marines have been a comparatively small, always elite force since their birth in a bar in Philly. For a variety of reasons, the Corps has amassed a record of combat victories that will be studied for millennia. The bottom line is, if you turn the Marines loose and tell them to get the job done however they can, the job will get done. It will likely be grotesquely bloody, gruesome, and graphic. The former armies of Japan, Germany, Iraq, North Korea, China, and many others would attest to this fact, but they can't because the Corps killed them. If Americans wants to win this war on terror, they will demand of the president and Congress that the Corps' end strength be dramatically increased and the Marines be given all the weapons and equipment they require. Then the progeny of Guadalcanal should be turned loose to do what they do best, no questions asked. When the job is done, the Marines will report this fact to the president, Congress, and people.

Anyone who has ever said war never solved anything has clearly never opened a history book. Wars have solved many major problems and, in fact, some wars prevent problems from becoming bigger problems. But don't tell a liberal or leftist any of this; reality and facts are deeply troubling to the hapless inhabitants of Fantasyland.

Our going to war with the Japanese and Germans in World War II prevented them from achieving their goal of global conquest. Our going to war against the North Koreans and Chinese kept South Korea free. Our going to war in Kuwait and Iraq in 1991 freed a peaceful nation and stopped Saddam from spreading his terror even further. Our going to war in Afghanistan severely damaged al Qaeda and brought down the murderous Taliban. And our going to war in Iraq in 2003 removed from power one of the worst mass murderers in history.

For various reasons, I've visited 43 countries in Asia, Europe, the Middle East, Oceania, Africa, and South and Central America since the 1970s, mostly during my 20 years in the Marine Corps. During those travels, I saw everything from decadent opulence and horrific strife to abject poverty and battlefields littered with literally hundreds and hundreds of burned and blown-apart bodies. And if there is one truism I learned while abroad, it is that there is no shortage of evil in the world, and that evil is always perpetrated by certified villains with Mephistophelian designs. Sadly, my Marines and I, despite our best intentions, have been allowed to kill only a tiny fraction of those so richly deserving of a painful, graphic death.

War sometimes not only solves horrendous problems, but it hones the fighting edge of combat forces, which if left to dull and rust, becomes a latent cancer that can quickly bring about disasters with untold consequences. Sometimes those consequences can lead to vastly increased suffering that could have been prevented by the swift deployment of a fearsome, elite force, such as the United States Marine Corps.

The wars in Afghanistan and Iraq are helping to build the leaders of tomorrow's Corps. The Marines nearly ran dry of combat-seasoned noncommissioned officers and officers in the last few years. The bedrock of the Marine Corps has always been salty leaders who have seen the elephant. Today's machine-gunner PFCs, mortar-gunner lance corporals, fire-team-leader corporals, platoon-commander lieutenants, and company-commander captains will be tomorrow's company gunnery sergeants, first sergeants, sergeants major, battalion commanders, and regimental commanders. Twenty years from now, young Marines will have these men lead them into combat knowing their leaders have been there and done that.

The Corps, which started off with a single recruiter posted inside Philadelphia's Tun Tavern with a mission of forming two battalions of Marines, as authorized by the Continental Congress, will press on as it always has—feared, respected, many say more than somewhat crazy, and always anxious to draw blood in the snow of far-off northern lands and in sunny tropic scenes. So albeit a grim fact, war also serves to steel the Marines of legend, who without this inevitable catalyst would long ago have faded into the shadows of history.

Have the Whiners Joined the Army?

Bitching among yourselves as military men is fine, so long as it does not get out of control, meaning it begins to effect unit readiness. Whining, on the other hand, especially to the press, is indicative of a unit with a leadership problem.

It was May 1991, and I was a platoon sergeant in a weapons platoon in a Marine infantry company. Standing in the hole in which I lived, I was dismayed that it was only May in the Kuwaiti desert, yet the temperature was well over 100 degrees Fahrenheit. The merciless sun beat down upon me and my Marines, none of whom were smiling. We had been in the zone since late 1990, had done our job by helping to destroy Saddam's army in Kuwait, and now we wanted to go home. Several times we had been given a date to get on the "freedom bird" to head back to Camp Lejeune (affectionately known to the Leathernecks of the vaunted 2nd Marine Division as Swamp Legloom), but each time we had been told the date had been pushed back. Every day, more and more snakes, camel spiders, and scorpions appeared in our holes to keep us company and keep us on our toes. Terrible dust storms blew in on a regular basis. The oil smoke from hundreds of burning oil wells choked and poisoned us. The chow stunk, good training was limited, wives and girlfriends were sending letters filled with anger and frustration at our continued absence, and there was no one left to kill (legally). Especially annoyed were some of the Marines who were being held over in the Corps past their end-of-active-service date because a "stop loss" policy had been instituted, meaning many of those who were slated to get out were still in.

Oh, and we bitched. Oh dear, did we bitch. We bitched to each other night and day. And there was plenty to bitch about, too. It is a Marine's God-given right to bitch, and it's been said many times that a Marine is not truly happy unless he has something to bitch about. Marines bitched on the island of New Providence in the Bahamas during the Revolutionary War. Marines bitched during the Boxer Rebellion in China. Marines bitched on Iwo Jima. Marines bitched at the Chosin Reservoir. Marines bitched at Khe Sanh. But two things Marines never do are bitch about fighting a war (they live for that) and bitch to the press. We keep our bitching to ourselves. Bitching to anyone else is unprofessional. Besides, what we bitch about is no one's business but our own.

The late author David Hackworth, a retired Army officer who was a 15-year-old soldier in World War II, wrote in a recent column about how many soldiers, even the legendary Green Berets, had been bitching to him about everything under the sun. This whining to the press is a very troubling development and tells me that some soldiers are now made from a different bolt of cloth than those who came before them. I have served with Green Berets and can assure you that the very idea of a Special Forces NCO (noncommissioned officer) crying like a little sissy-boy to the media because he's hot or he's cold or he misses his family was unthinkable back in the proverbial day.

Unit morale problems are always an indication of a leadership failure. If what Hackworth said is true and Green Berets are crying to him, the Army needs to determine which units are suffering from poor leadership and move to fix that problem before it spreads like the malicious virus it is.

In the interim, suck it up, soldier, lest the ghost of Patton slap you upside your head.

Set Loose the Beast of Belleau Wood

Combat experience is one of the most valuable tools in the Corps' considerable arsenal. The Corps has known this for centuries. There are few military organizations whose records of combat success equal that of the United States Marine Corps, and enemies of the Corps are usually aware of this.

A recent caller to the "Gunny Bob Show" who had served in the U.S. Army in Operation Iraqi Freedom said that the Marines he saw operating in combat in Iraq were "insane," which to a Marine is a high compliment. This insanity is, of course, not insanity but rather extreme aggression on the battlefield, which oftentimes frightens the enemy badly enough that he hesitates and begins to question his career choice. That moment of hesitation and doubt is frequently a primary reason why the Marines win the day against grim odds.

History speaks to us of certain great fighting forces led by men upon whom legends are based.

In American military history, there is no armed force equal to the band of seagoing savages known as the United States Marine Corps. Indeed, the very uttering by a hapless opponent of this force's name has been known to cause instant panic followed by an undignified retreat, for to stand

and face the descendants of the *teufelhunden* [1] of Belleau Wood (where Marines defeated some Germans in France in a fierce battle) is to invite sure, graphic death. We're going to kill you and that's that.

The Corps' celebrated history is filled with colorful characters with names like Smedley "Ol' Gimlet Eye" Butler, Leland D. "Crow" Crawford, Dan Daly, John Quick, Gregory "Pappy" Boyington, Archibald Henderson, Leland "Lou" Diamond, "Manila John" Basilone, and the quasi-mythical Lewis B. "Chesty" Puller, the latter of whom won five Navy Crosses and to whom, every night at lights out in boot camp, Marine recruits say, "Good night, Chesty, wherever you are." These men and innumerable other Marine heroes fought in such places as Iwo Jima, the Chosin Reservoir, Khe Sanh, Guadalcanal, and Hue.

After Vietnam, the Corps' foundation of noncommissioned, staff noncommissioned, and commissioned officers with combat experience slowly began to deteriorate for lack of a major war. An unfortunate fact is that between 1975 (the fall of Vietnam) and 1991 (the Gulf War), only a small percentage of the Corps was lucky enough to see combat in such engagements as Beirut, Grenada, and Panama. In fact, the last time the Corps had a Sergeant Major of the Marine Corps who rated the Combat Action Ribbon was the summer of 1999. (It is troubling to many Marines to have privates, PFCs, and lance corporals with extensive combat time and a Sergeant Major of the Marine Corps with none. This does not mean a Sergeant Major of the Marine Corps with no combat time whatsoever can't lead Marines, but what it does mean to many Marines is that the Corps' senior enlisted man can't personally relate to Marines far his junior when it comes to killing.)

The Gulf War, albeit short-lived, helped the Corps' lead-

1. German for "devil dog."

ers regain some of the vital seasoning that comes with punch-ups. Somalia and the Balkans came along, but again, comparatively few Marines saw action in those operations.

Then it was back to the "sandbox" in the spring of 2003, and the Marine Corps once again demonstrated why, in the end, it is always sheer folly to test one's mettle against these men whose forefathers, from the island of New Providence in the Bahamas [2] to and beyond the bloody streets of Mogadishu, taught bitter lessons to doomed enemies. (If you choose to go up against a unit like 3rd Battalion, 4th Marines, led by Lieutenant Colonel Bryan P. McCoy for two tours in Iraq, you are a dead man, plain and simple. With very light casualties, this unit alone killed staggering numbers of Iraqi troops, guerrillas, and terrorists in the march to Baghdad and giant slugfests in places like Fallajuh.)

Now there's talk among Democrats about reinstating the draft. We need no draft, which can create major quality-control problems. What we need is a substantially larger Marine Corps. The Congress should immediately approve the Corps' end strength to be increased to, say, 225,000 instead of the current strength of about 175,000. Training, equipping, and assigning (not to mention eventually deploying) an extra 50,000 Marines would take some time and a lot of money, but failing to do so would cost us all the more in the long run. Or, better yet, activate the entire 4th Marine Division and 4th Marine Air Wing (the Marine Corps Reserve), which consist of Marines already trained and equipped, many of whom have combat experience.

The sooner we do this, the better, and the sooner the Corps can add streamers for Iran and Syria to its battle colors.

2. The Continental Marines' first amphibious invasion. In March 1776 in a 13-day operation, Marines captured two British forts, seized Government House, occupied Nassau, and captured 88 guns.

From Brushfires to Conflagrations

Living in the American West, one quickly learns that brushfires can quickly turn into huge forest fires if they are not quickly contained and extinguished. The same holds true for the war on terror in that failure to quickly identify and contain the threat will likely result in a conflagration of potentially global proportions.

Bill Clinton ignored this fact.

Based in the Pacific in the 1970s, I was assigned my first billet involving defeating terrorists, with the heavy hitters being groups like Yasser Arafat's Palestine Liberation Organization (PLO) and the New People's Army. [1] In Europe in the early and mid-1980s, my daily duties included, among other things, avoiding being blown up by the Communist Combatant Cells, [2] Red Army Faction, [3] Action Direct, [4] ETA, [5] and the Red Brigades, [6] among other terrorist groups. (Also during this time, the United States suffered horrendous losses to terrorists in the Middle East.) By the late 1980s, I found myself teaching counterterrorism at a classified Department of Defense school, during which time a Marine gunnery sergeant was assassinated by a "sparrow squad" from the Marxist New People's Army in the Philippines. Also assassinated by a sparrow squad was U.S. Army Medal of Honor recipient Col. James "Nick" Rowe.

The author (third from the left) with his Recon team in the Philippines, circa 1980. Author's photo.

As you know, in early 1990, I suggested to the editor of the *Marine Corps Gazette* (a professional education journal of the Corps) that the magazine publish an article on how terrorism was going to be a major threat to Americans in the coming years and that Marines would be fighting terrorists more and more. You also know he wrote back saying I didn't know what I was talking about and that the Corps would never become a force that would frequently find itself engaging terrorists.

Institutional arrogance and a failure (unwillingness?) to understand the nature of the terrorist beast are two of the most commonplace assets terrorists use against us. These factors contribute directly to the growth of terrorist movements, which always begin as infants but which more and more frequently grow into maturity with alarming rapidity.

If the civilized world does not act upon this fact in the very near future, brushfire wars involving terrorists will evolve into full-blown conflagrations that will spread with horrific speed that we will be unable to douse.

For example, the New People's Army was once a smallish band of communist thugs. Today, they are tens of thousands strong and represent a dire threat to the Philippines.

In Nepal, the communist terrorists there began as a minor rebellion in the mid-1990s. They have now slaughtered many thousands and can shut down the capital of Katmandu at will.

In the late 1960s, Basque terrorists known as ETA began a modest terrorist campaign for independence. Now more than 800 people have been killed in attacks in this European nation.

Islamic terrorism began with the PLO and has been allowed to fester and become so grim an infection that Muslim terrorists now have the ability to strike in nearly any country.

As the United States continues to rebuild and refashion its military from being disemboweled by negligent politicians and a complacent populace in the 1990s, we must look at successful counterterrorist programs (the British against the Irish Republican Army and communist terrorists in then Malaya, the Germans against the Red Army Faction, the Italians against the Red Brigades, the Peruvians against Sendero Luminoso, [7] et al) and apply the lessons learned there to the current situation.

If one examines the aforementioned successes, two obvious facts are revealed: the good guys engaged the bad guys early on and kept at it very vigorously, refusing to surrender and attacking the enemy every way they could, everywhere they could.

If we fail to do the same, more and more brushfires will erupt into firestorms of unspeakable intensity, and all the water in the world won't be nearly enough to stop them.

Unfortunately, many Americans don't believe in prescribed burns or proactively thinning out forests, and it is these Americans the terrorists are counting on.

1. The terrorist arm of the Communist Party of the Philippines.

2. A Belgium-based communist terrorist group founded by Pierre Carette.

3. Formed from the Baader-Meinhof Gang, the RAF was a Marxist-Maoist terrorist group that operated in Europe from the 1970s until the 1990s.

4. A Greece-based anti-American terrorist group.

5. Spain's homegrown Basque terrorist group.

6. Italy's communist terrorist group.

7. Peru's communist terrorist group led by Abimael Guzman. *Sendero Luminoso* is Spanish for "Shining Path."

Send in the Clowns

Good reporting on the war on terror should include using sources to break stories without endangering lives. News consumers and competing journalists sometimes become frustrated when one journalist amasses a record of successes along these lines that cannot be matched.

Two of the most frequent questions I am asked regarding my work as a military science and terrorism analyst are: "Why are your analyses and predictions so accurate so often?" and "How are you able to break so many stories before anyone else?"

Granted, some of the stories I've broken—which are oftentimes picked up by the mainstream media weeks, months, even more than a year later and reported as if *they* just broke the story—manage to stun certain people and organizations.

One such story was when I reported U.S. submarines were clandestinely posted off the coast of North Korea with orders to stand by to sink any ship exiting a North Korean port that intelligence said was carrying illicit nuclear weapons technology or components to another rogue state, such as Iran. (Saying U.S. subs are operating in a certain ocean or sea is not releasing classified information and in no way endangered any submarine.) This blew a lot of people's minds because it meant I knew where some of our subs were, what their mission was, and that the president had authorized the Pentagon to, upon his orders, instruct their crews to commit an act of war at any moment upon a country with which we were not at war. Three months after I reported this situation, a Japanese newspaper verified it upon interviewing one of the U.S. envoys involved in the multilateral talks between the North and South Koreans, Japanese, Chinese, Russians, and Americans.

I was immediately asked how I knew the president of the United States had secretly decided to make it U.S. policy to sink commercial vessels believed to be ferrying nuclear arms material between North Korea and an illegal buyer.

I've bugged the Oval Office, of course.

Not really. I have methods and sources, just like any other investigative journalist. It's just that mine are better than most.

OK, so I have publicly broken numerous stories and made dozens of accurate analyses and predictions in the war on terror since October 2001. Why are so many people so amazed at this? There are many people who are very good at their jobs, which are jobs I have absolutely no idea how to do and, frankly, might very well never be able to learn.

I mean, a friend of mine is a retired scientist who helped make a probe fly through a comet's tail to collect data. Now how the hell did he do that?

My point—and I do have one—is that if you have decades of experience doing a certain thing, and if many others in the same line of work simply can't match your record of success, their weaknesses tend to make you look even brighter.

Maybe you have detected them and maybe you haven't, but the media is packed with pretenders who have conned their way in front of cameras and microphones by padding their CVs and developing a slick delivery to those who don't know any better.

So it's not that I am some sort of war-on-terror soothsayer; far from it. It's just that I am very fortunate to have been given opportunities many others never received, and I've learned how to parlay that experience into information people want. Typical Marine Corps self-confidence and initiative haven't hurt, either. And if the media keeps sending in the aforementioned clowns, who speak in broad generalities and know how to dazzle the easily impressed with glittery but meaningless military jargon, I will no doubt continue to look all the more clever, for which I must thank the rubes with whom I share the airwaves, ink, and cyberspace.

Darkside to Paris: The French Await Their Gruesome Fate (Again)

Camaraderie and brotherhood are two of the Corps' many weapons that have been toted onto battlefields from the Barbary Coast to al Qaim. When two Marines are "tight," they can oftentimes communicate across vast distances using what appears to be some sort of extrasensory perception.

The call came tonight as I sat in front of my computer wondering what to write about.

Darkside has always come through like that.

Lieutenant Colonel Bryan P. "Darkside" McCoy, United States Marine Corps, was at the other end. You now know he is the Marine who ordered the now famous tearing down of the statue of Saddam in Baghdad's Firdos Square. Bryan and I are old friends from another lifetime in the 2nd Marine Division; I was his company gunnery sergeant and he was my company commander. "Darkside" was his radio call sign in Iraq. Author John Koopman's new book, *McCoy's Marines: Darkside to Baghdad*, is where his call sign gained notoriety. (The book's cover features Bryan's filthy war visage with a Cohiba cigar clamped in it. One look at that mug, that "war face" in the Corps' lexicon, and you know he means to do great harm to anyone stupid enough to face him.)

"Bob," he said after I said hello.

"Yeah?" came my suspicious reply. (The caller ID had failed.)

"McCoy."

"Bryan!" I shouted. In the corner of my left eye I could see my wife smile.

The best officer who had ever commanded me wanted to shoot the breeze and tell me about a writing project he had been assigned as a student in a school for senior military officers. He wanted to give me the basics of the lengthy paper and warn me that he was sending it to me for my "chop." Of course, there will be little if anything I could add, as Bryan surely doesn't need me to edit his paper. But he has always used me, and a tiny group of other staff noncommissioned officers he knows, as sounding boards. That's one of the character traits that make him so dangerous to people he wants to kill.

Reunion. The author (left) with Lieutenant Colonel Bryan P. McCoy USMC at the author's home, summer 2004. Author's photo.

Last summer he stopped by on his way from California to Washington after leading his battalion through two tours in Iraq in the most brutal combat the Corps had seen since Vietnam. We sat out back in the comfort and general pleasantness of my backyard. We ate, drank, and smoked cigars. I got him to do most of the talking because, although I, too, am a combat veteran of the Corps, what he had just gone through twice was beyond my experience.

Tonight's call also included news that he is heading to France on his school's debate team to debate the French military.

I managed to compose myself after a few moments and asked why the Corps would do something so evil as to send its most impolitic, vicious killer to a place like France to debate that hapless country's embarrassing military. His modesty made him change the topic.

That's Bryan.

Selected for promotion to colonel, this summer he accepted a position developing combat training for the Corps. It is a perfect billet for him between wars. The Marines he will train will be substantially more professional killers having been trained by Bryan. His new job is the worst possible news for current and future enemies of America.

I pity the French, who will be tormented and humiliated by this modern-day Genghis Khan.

And no one will be able to help the doomed dregs he next faces on the field of battle, in some distant clime and place.

A Fundamental Fact of War with Fundamentalists

Understanding one's enemy is crucial to victory. Sadly, many Americans do not understand our current enemy, nor do they want to. The enemy is counting on this fact, which adds to his combat power.

There's nothing so clarifying as standing among hundreds of dead bodies.

I've had to do that a couple of times: once in 1983 when I was the Marine Corps' liaison to the FBI forensics team working to identify 241 dead men who had perished in Beirut at the hands of Hezbollah, [1] and the second time in Kuwait on the Highway to Hell, where hundreds of Iraqi soldiers paid the ultimate price for their crimes against humanity in a grisly, miles-long jumble of mangled vehicles on the road between Kuwait City and Basra. (Sometimes nightmares of the Beirut bodies haunt me, but the Highway to Hell bodies never invade my sleep, I suppose because the latter were scum-sucking bottom feeders who got what was coming to them.) Experiences such as these clarify things in one's mind

1. An Islamic terrorist group supported by the governments of Iran and Syria and currently locked in a death struggle with Israel.

because it reveals a basic truism many Americans still cannot—and perhaps never will—grasp. That truism is that we are at war with fundamental Islam.

Many Americans can't or won't understand this, some because they are simply too stupid or naïve to get a grip on the fact that we are at war with a monster that wants every American man, woman, and child dead, and others because of their blinding hatred for a president who is quite clearly willing to do his duty. In a weird sort of way, our enemy loves those who love John Kerry.

The slaughter at a school in southern Russia should not have come as a surprise to anyone, but it no doubt did to some. I first began warning in the fall of 2001 that Muslim terrorists would target schools filled with children. Some self-proclaimed terrorism analysts also in the media disagreed with me, saying terrorists would not intentionally target kids because of the negative publicity. These pundits fail to understand the underlying tenet of terrorism, which is that any publicity is good publicity when that publicity is seen by certain factions as Islam striking back at who tens of millions of Muslims perceive as their enemy. And their perceived enemy's children, according to scores of Muslim clerics around the world (and governments like those of Syria and Iran), are just as legitimate and valuable a target as adults.

Why? Because those children are not only the spawn of infidel evil, but they will soon grow into adulthood, from which additional evil, such as Western influence, concepts, values, and principles, will come.

The greatest fear of fundamentalist Islam is that the West will reveal this hoard to be precisely that: a maniacal mob of feral fiends in league with Beelzebub. Yet it matters not to many Americans how many innocents die gruesome deaths at the hands of these killers, for some politically correct, sensitive Americans (and one presidential candidate), and perhaps even more Europeans of the same ilk, fatally insist on believing we can talk these brutes out of it. Nevertheless, reality tells those who will listen to reason that, just as you can't talk a black mamba out of chasing you down and biting you, nor can you talk fascist jihadists out of it. They've gone after Israeli children and now Russian children. Eventually American children will be targeted. Those who don't believe that are fools. France and now Russia have learned how strategically unsound it is to refuse to fight terrorists abroad, for reports say 10 of the schoolyard terrorists were Arabs; hired guns on loan from al Qaeda. Will we, too, succumb to pressure from the foolhardy left to pull back?

Our enemy understands two things: pain and death. Given this undeniable fact, if we are to prevent this festering faction of Islam from repeating their heinous deeds of Beslan on American soil, we must stand and deliver horrific pain and grim death to their doorstep, regardless of where that doorstep is found and regardless of what the corrupt and morally bankrupt United Nations has to say about it.

At this point, it is literally us or them.

Who will it be?

A New Carpet for Iran's Atomic Genie?

As a student of Iran since 1979, I've taken note of many grim developments at the behest of that nation's terrorist government. Now, not only does Iran have the capability to accurately strike anywhere in the Middle East, but they are deeply involved in funneling high-tech weapons and detonation systems into Iraq, as more and more American and British forces know all too well.

If you thought we had enough to worry about with Iran's nuclear weapons development program, and if you thought we had enough to worry about when it comes to a fairly likely repeat presidential candidate with a long and sordid history of weakening our nation's military, homeland security, and intelligence capabilities (hmmm; now am I talking about Kerry or Hillary?), think again. Iran's nuclear genie may have a new carpet.

Comments made by Ali Shamkhani, Iran's defense minister, after what was believed to be the testing of an upgraded Shahab-3 [1] ballistic missile, got my attention and that of

1. The Shahab-3 is based upon North Korea's No-Dong missile, which was created with Soviet and Chinese technical assistance and Iranian funding.

certain other military and terrorism analysts. His comments mentioned increased range, among other things. And intelligence sources who keep an ear to the ground in that region are now hearing talk about exactly what Shamkhani was alluding to, namely, that Iran may have acquired—most likely from Korea, if true—the Shahab-5 or 6 booster package for the Shahab-3 system. If this is correct, what does it mean strategically?

Well, it ain't good. If Iran has managed to come up with the Shahab-6 booster, it means that the terrorist government of Iran now has the ability to reach not only any target it so desires in all of the Middle East (the Global Positioning System targeting technology the Clinton administration sold the Chinese is responsible for Iran's Shahabs being so much more accurate now; the Chinese either sold this technology directly to Iran or used North Korea as a middleman), but now all of Europe. That's right. If Iran has the Shahab-6, with the GPS navigation and targeting system that we know they already have, Iran can accurately strike embassies, nuclear power plants, military bases, city centers, government complexes (how does Parliament sound?), port facilities, NATO headquarters, and any other target it so desires anywhere in Europe. But perhaps even more valuable than the ability to do so would be Iran's ability to threaten to do so with such a threat not being a bluff but a demonstrated fact.

Oh, but wait. It gets worse.

Some intelligence analysts are now openly worried that Iran may be further ahead in the nuclear weapons development program than originally thought. Conventional wisdom had been saying that Iran would be able to field a nuclear warhead in 2006. If Israel or the United States do not interdict Iran's nuke program soon, we may find out the hard way if all this is true.

And Israel might very well beat us to the punch. A while

back I reported the 100-percent unclassified story of Israel's buying a large selection of precision bunker-buster bombs from the United States, which might be able to penetrate Iran's hardened underground nuclear facilities. My report was confirmed months later by the mainstream media (glad to see said media is on the ball).

In the words of the Wicked Witch of the West as she soaked up a bucket of water, "What a world, what a world . . . "

Twisted Steel and Licorice

Most Americans, I suspect, envision Marines as diabolical, half-mad killers who average 6 feet 3 inches tall, crush the scale at 250 pounds of muscle and sinew, and have absolutely no feelings for anyone or anything except their weapons and fellow Marines.

He still isn't old enough to have a beer, but in his two decades of life, the young Marine is already about to complete his second tour in Iraq. To the combat-hardened veteran, it seems like yesterday that he was traipsing through an alder patch with his Labrador and shotgun in the hamlet of Warren, Maine, where he grew up. Now and then, he wonders how he so quickly went from hunting partridge off of Patterson Mill Road to hunting men along Haifa Street.

The Leatherneck, however, like so many of his brothers, is an anomaly made of twisted steel and licorice. A cold-blooded killer who doesn't have time for regret, he loves giving cherry licorice whips to the Iraqi children who come out of their homes to watch the Marines on patrol. Their big, brown eyes remind him of his kid sister's eyes, whom he hasn't seen in—in a long time. In the small part of his heart that will always remain innocent, he yearns to again hear the gleeful laughs of his siblings as they chase the family Lab around the yard that overlooks Crawford Pond.

He is usually happy. Two things in particular make him smile: receiving letters and packages from home, and listening to the continual banter of his brother Marines.

But today he is confused, though not surprised. In a package from home were several American newspapers. Each told stories of how the Iraqis hated the Americans and how car bombs and terrorists were likely to destroy the upcoming election and even lose the war. He wonders why the news doesn't report all the good things that are happening in Iraq now that Saddam is in prison and how so many Iraqis come up to them and thank them.

"Hey, Land Shark," he says to his friend, calling him by his nickname. "It says here we are losing the war. This Senator Boxer chick says we suck."

"Yeah, right. Maybe that newspaper and Senator Boxer should tell that to all the dead terrorists we did last night, right man?" Land Shark replies.

"Mmmm," comes the nodded reply. "Hey, you're from California. When we get back to the world, maybe you should knock on her door, tell her you're delivering a love note from Saddam, and then bite her head off when she opens it."

"Nah. Why should I soil my beautiful teeth?" Land Shark smiles back, revealing the grin of a movie star, which miraculously remains intact despite the horrific scar running from the Marine's right eyebrow down across his nose to the tip of his chin. Shrapnel tends to leave calling cards like that. Land Shark hopes the chicks will dig it when he gets back to the world. (Land Shark had been worried that his sister's high school graduation gift to him, a teeth-whitening session from BriteSmile, was going to be ruined.)

The Marine folds up the newspaper and picks up his rifle as he watches his unit begin to make final preparations for tonight's patrol. His "company gunny" is walking around reminding the Marines to make sure they each have an extra tourniquet in the right cargo pocket of their trousers.

In his mind's eye, for a moment he is back in Medomak Valley High School, holding Kathy's hand during lunch. His beautiful girlfriend, he knows, is still waiting for him back in Warren. When he gets out of the Corps, they will marry and he will become a lobsterman and moor his boat in Spruce Head Island Harbor. The buoys of his lobster traps will decorate the Atlantic's surface around granite islands like Matinicus, Wooden Ball, and Monhegan.

As he slips on his flak jacket and checks to see if the package of licorice is still in the jacket's left pocket, the Marine doesn't know that she will wait forever, for he won't be returning from tonight's patrol.

Phantoms of the Fifth Column

The Marine sniper is among the most deadly weapons systems on the battlefield. He is trained to do things most would think impossible. If he has you in his sights and you run, you will only die tired.

Like a wraith on a Welsh moor he comes, cloaked in the inky night. Clutched in his talon-like hands he holds his instrument of reckoning. Made of steel and fiberglass, it is as much a part of the man as is the man's own heart, which beats calmly in his chest.

His eyes shine in the trickle of smoke-shrouded moonlight that makes its way from the heavens down to the ravaged landscape of the city.

They are the eyes of a predator: sure, steady, knowing, purposeful.

The hunter moves with his shadow; another man with another rifle who, like his brother, seems more catlike than human.

Approaching the low wall that lines the edge of the rooftop, the duo comes to a synchronized stop with no words spoken between them. They are two men who need no words to communicate, for their minds speak to each other on a plane of consciousness few others will ever know. With fine-tuned ears trained to filter out the extraneous and lock onto the relevant, they listen but detect nothing of immediate concern.

Again without speaking, the two move into a corner that forms a shadow. It is a natural place from which the pair hopes to strike.

One man removes a dark piece of cloth from his pack and covers the barrel of the other man's rifle, which is now pointed out over the top of the low wall and down the long street below their hide. The cloth appears to be just a discarded rag as it hides the barrel's presence.

For five hours the men wait. The only parts of their body that move in that time are their breathing chests and blinking eyelids.

Finally, two hours before the first rays of dawn begin to streak the sky, their prey appears from a car nearly 1,000 yards distant. The two men remove a large object from the vehicle and place the improvised explosive device beside a light post and quickly move back towards the car.

The first shot strikes the lead man in the side of the head, killing him instantly as half of his skull is flung into the street. The second terrorist turns instinctively toward the rifle's distant bark and begins to raise his own weapon, but the wraith's second messenger of death is already inbound. It catches the other bomber square in the chest—center mass. The man's heart explodes as the bullet tears out his back and comes to a stop embedded in the wall behind him. A third shot hits the bomb, which explodes instantly.

On the rooftop, for a fleeting moment you might have thought you saw a shadow moving toward a doorway. Was it your mind playing tricks on you? Your searching eyes see nothing now. The wraiths are gone, if they were ever there.

The brothers—a Marine Corps scout-sniper team—have

vanished into the night. Phantoms of the fifth column, [1] they will return to their daylight lair to rest and eat and clean their weapons. Tomorrow night, while you sleep in the warm comfort of your bed, they will again slink through the darkness to hunt the orcs [2] of Baghdad.

1. During the Spanish Civil War (1936-39), as Nationalist General Emilio Mola Vidal was marching his four columns toward Madrid, he referred to his guerrillas in Madrid as his "fifth column."

2. A reference to J.R.R. Tolkien's savage, ugly creatures that so pestered certain men, hobbits, elves, a dwarf, and a wizard in Middle Earth.

Corporal Smuckatelli Comes Calling

If you have ever wanted to meet and get to know a Marine, here's your chance.

Not long ago, he jumped off of his tractor on the farm back in Nebraska. He closed and locked the door to his construction office in Boston. He parked his big rig out behind the garage in Miami and hopped out. He shut down his computer in East L.A. He stacked the last lobster pot on the dock beside his boat in Thomaston, Maine. He closed on the final mortgage of the day in Denver. And he kissed his wife and children good-bye. He then put on his helmet, slid into his flak jacket, casually whipped his 100-pounds-plus pack onto his muscular back, picked up his weapon and ammo, and shot his way into history, leaving a trail of enemy bodies behind him from the halls of Montezuma and the shores of Tripoli to the carcass-littered streets of Fallujah.

His name is Corporal Smuckatelli.

He is a young man, but he is old beyond his years. Death is his constant companion. The lines and scars etched into his face will not fade with time. His bright eyes shine at night like those of a leopard stalking some hapless prey. Filthy, exhausted, and oftentimes bleeding, he doesn't give a damn about what some Hollywood has-been or caterwauling trio of Dixie dimwits has to say about this, that, or the other thing. He thinks only of one thing: accomplishing his mission with as many of his brother Marines still alive as possible. Thoughts of his family must wait until the job is done.

He's a killer. As cold-blooded as they come, he doesn't concern himself with the grim deeds he has done. There will be time for reflection later, but tears for the enemy will not be part of those afterthoughts. His tears he saves for his brothers who fell and not for those who foolishly opposed his will, for the enemy had it coming. Smuckatelli knows the enemy seeks martyrdom, and he is happy to arrange his opponent's journey into the netherworld. Perhaps later in life, maybe in his middle-aged years, he will wake in a cold sweat screaming night after night. But the screams will not be an accounting for what he did in the war. They will be for his long-dead brothers and for Marines once again facing the beast. He prays he led and trained them well enough in earlier wars. He knows those he led in war in another lifetime are now the leaders themselves. He shouts orders and encouragement at the television when he sees Marines in combat. Yes, he knows they can't hear him. Combat is quite loud, you see.

November 10 is his birthday. He is 230 years old but doesn't look a day over 200. On 10 November 1775, the Continental Congress authorized the formation of two battalions of Marines. Little did those first Marines know that their Corps' future would see them in every clime and place, from the Peking Legation, Belleau Wood, the Chosin Reservoir, and Guadalcanal to Khe Sanh, Beirut, Mogadishu, and Baghdad. Smuckatelli was there from the beginning.

Your country stands in awe of you, Corporal Smuckatelli, and the myriad battles you have fought and won. I, too, marvel at what you have done, and you know I wish I could be with you today. Although you don't require the services of Gunny Newman anymore, my prayers are with you, and that's pretty good ammo.

God bless the Marines. Long live the Corps. Death to those who oppose us and may our enemies' souls suffer in the bowels of hell for eternity.

Adventures Across the Spectrum of Conflict

I first heard the term Spectrum of Conflict back in the 1980s. Little did I know then that my future would include a great deal of study about the spectrum. And I certainly never imagined that I would one day be writing about it. The Spectrum of Conflict is a good means for learning about the nature of various forms of warfare. This chapter is a brief lesson.

I was an odd child, with an early indication of my oddity being my annoying demand for history teachers to discuss (after class) tactics, operational art, and strategy as practiced by warriors from the legions of Rome to Marine rifle squads in the War in the Pacific. So it was no surprise to my family and teachers to one day learn I had joined the Marines.

As a "warfighting" instructor during my last tour in the Corps before retirement, I taught, among other topics, the spectrum of conflict, which details the differences between types of warfare. For example, toward the bottom of the scale are "low-intensity conflicts" or LICs, such as home-grown guerrilla insurgencies, and at the top of the scale is global thermonuclear war. In teaching about the spectrum, I always stressed the importance of selecting LICs to prosecute by determining if that LIC is in our national strategic interest and if we have a good chance of winning. Sadly, these are two factors that American supporters of Saddam Hussein, Osama bin Laden, and others who pose a threat to our survival don't get.

I am frequently asked by said supporters (also known as "Bush haters" and "fools") why, now that we have liberated Iraq from Saddam, we do not attack all tyrants and terrorists everywhere.

The reason, I explain to these transparent simpletons, is that such a game plan is politically, logistically, tactically, operationally, and strategically impossible, and that not all tyrants and terrorists are serious threats to Americans and America. I also point out that a nation must prioritize its military engagements.

So, when the wild-eyed leftists ask me why we don't invade North Korea, I explain that the North Koreans are strongly believed to have nuclear weapons that can reach not only Seoul and Tokyo but the West Coast of the United States, the residents of which would prefer not be on the receiving end of a retaliatory strike by North Korea. They become very confused when I explain that wars should be last resorts, that North Korea is still negotiating with us (off and on), and that they have no plans to launch a preemptive nuclear strike on us or our allies.

The liberals really hate it when U.S. military action removes a maniacal, genocidal savage like Hussein and brutal regimes like the Taliban. And the wacko left goes bonkers when such actions result in terrorist-tyrants like Libya's Ghadafi publicly quitting the WMD game, not wanting to be next on our list of scum to be dealt with once and for all. The left cringes when one successful war leads to another, which results in a third war being avoided but a threat nevertheless being neutralized.

Many liberals are screaming that because we liberated

Iraq and Afghanistan, we should also have to invade Haiti and Congo, neither of which is a threat to the United States or Americans, nor our allies abroad, and neither of which is of strategic interest to us. That's the cold way of the world, and nothing's going to change that.

We need to continue selecting the right targets at the right times and ignore the maniac leftists who live in Fantasyland, where Howard Dean is their socialist king, having replaced the fallen (for the time being?) John Kerry.

If the radical left comes to power in 2008, as bin Laden is desperately hoping, we will pay dearly in the spectrum of conflict.

Hang on to your helmet.

The Dangerous Folly of the Other-Guy Syndrome

Many people rely on luck and the odds to get by. Those who rely upon common sense, pro-active actions, and an understanding of reality tend to live longer, generally speaking. This chapter explains it all.

It usually happens to the other guy.

What usually happens to the other guy? Everything, of course. I mean, the odds of something bad happening to you—getting hit by a train, choking to death on a chicken bone, getting audited by the Internal Revenue Service, taking a poison dart in the neck—are slim, so wouldn't it be smarter, at least fiscally, to just play the odds, cross your fingers, and hope for the best?

This is obviously the way most of corporate America, as well as municipal and state governments, are playing the (for lack of a better phrase) game of terrorism prevention. Sure, lots of folks died on 9-11, and al Qaeda has been successful in other nasty attacks, such as the Bali nightclub and Jakarta Marriott bombings. But al Qaeda, by sheer odds alone in a target-rich world, is unlikely to strike you, your family, your friends, or your business. Chances are, the other guy is going to get it.

The problem is, to the other guy, *you* are the other guy.

I've conducted quite a few vulnerability assessments since 9-11 on such targets as airports (commercial and general aviation), city centers, ground mass transit, fuel farms (those giant gas and oil tanks), ports, hotels, tourist attractions, schools, and so on, and I regret to inform you that corporate America and city and state governments have done nowhere near enough to even seriously begin defending against the next al Qaeda or other terrorist-group attacks. These entities are instead falling prey to the "Other-Guy Syndrome."

If I could tell you just some of the things I know when it comes to how close we have come since 9-11, and if I could tell you just some of the horrifying things al Qaeda and other bad guys are hoping to pull off in the near future, you would book a seat on the next flight to Mars or, barring that, would be packing your bags for a mountaintop in Antarctica. Yes, it is that bad, and it is only a matter of time before someone, somewhere, is able to pull off another spectacular mass-casualty attack on Americans, either right here at home or abroad.

The frustrating part of all this is how simple, cost-effective measures could prevent such an attack, especially when carried out by companies, industries, and governments staffed by realists who know better than to play this incredibly dangerous game and who take their duties seriously.

Airports, planes, high-rise buildings, trains, pro sports venues, schools, government offices, military bases, churches, synagogues, hazardous waste sites and transport systems, refineries, power plants, bridges, dams, and so many more targets in Colorado and across the country remain shockingly undefended, frequently because those responsible for protecting them are rolling the dice and hoping that, if something does happen, it will happen to the other guy.

And when the next attacks come, those who could have done something to prevent the attacks will blame everyone except themselves.

Welcome to America, land of the free and home of the complacent and negligent.

Those Pesky Missing Weapons of Mass Destruction

Fine. So our intel on Iraq's WMDs appears at the moment to have been off the mark. Does that mean we commit suicide? No. It means we had better take the required measures to make damn sure our intel dramatically improves.

The overriding reason President George Bush gave for removing Saddam Hussein from power were his weapons of mass destruction, which our intelligence and that of Great Britain promised us Saddam still had and was in fact hiding. It has now painfully clear that those WMDs may not be found in any great quantities inside Iraq.

The result of this is four camps: (1) those who think Bush, British Prime Minister Tony Blair, Australian Prime Minister John Howard, and numerous other Western leaders lied about the intelligence, (2) those who think our intelligence may have been wrong, (3) those who think the WMDs are still there or nearby but have yet to be found, and (4) those who don't care about the WMDs because Saddam, who murdered more than one million men, women, and children during his horrific reign, should have been deposed with or without WMDs.

In retrospect, it would have been wiser for Bush and

Blair to not rest their case so heavily on the WMDs almost to the exclusion of other valid reasons for Hussein's forced unemployment. There were plenty, too, besides the mind-blowing number of people he butchered in crimes against humanity few Americans can even begin to comprehend, some of whose remains (estimated at 300,000) are now being dug up in hundreds of mass graves. There were his nightmarish torture chambers, where atrocities beyond description, frequently involving parents being forced to watch their children suffer horrifying acts of mayhem, were daily entertainment for Saddam, his sons, and their maniacal henchmen. There was Saddam's plotted assassination of former President George Herbert Walker Bush after the Gulf War. There was Saddam's refusal to abide by the terms of surrender his regime signed in 1991, which eventually led to an embarrassing number of violations of United Nations resolutions by Saddam between 1991 and 2003, virtually including throwing out UN weapons inspectors in 1998 (the UN did nothing effective about these violations, of course). There were his aforementioned direct ties to terrorism, including his support of al Qaeda's Ansar al Islam biological weapons research facility and terrorist training camp inside Iraq, his long-time support of Baghdad resident Abu Nidal (of the Abu Nidal Organization; 300 dead in more than 20 countries, including attacks on Americans and a Pan Am airliner in Karachi) who died in 2002, and Baghdad resident Abu Abbas (captured 50 miles west of Baghdad by U.S. troops in April 2003) of the Palestine Liberation Front, who masterminded the 1985 hijacking of the cruise ship *Achille Lauro*, leaving 69-year-old invalid and American citizen Leon Klinghoffer dead. And there was his public penchant for sending huge sums of money directly into the Palestinian terror machine.

But none of these outrages troubled an ethically corrupt and morally bankrupt UN enough to act.

So, if massive quantities of WMDs exist, where are they? Hans Blix, Madeleine Albright, Kofi Annan, and Hillary Clinton, a foursome of Bush haters, have each admitted the WMDs could be in the hands of terrorists. Let's hope they are wrong.

And let this lesson serve to remind presidents that even the best intelligence sometimes comes up short.

End of Days: When America Falls

Pay no attention to raving lunatics like Pat Robertson, who continue to claim that the end of mankind is at hand because earthquakes, floods, hurricanes, and tsunamis appear to be on the increase. Instead, I recommend you focus on the problems America is causing for itself, which could lead to our downfall long, long before the reign of man is terminated.

No country can last forever. Yes, a country's name might remain the same, but types of government eventually change, such as with England and China, which means the country that was is gone, although the people and national moniker might remain.

History reveals three primary reasons why countries fall, governments change, and ways of life vanish.

The Taliban, Saddam, Nazis, and many other governments fell because of *war with other nations.*

Revolutions brought on by internal strife, an insurgency, social unrest and disillusionment, reduced respect and admiration of the nation's military (note that the Marines and Army are occasionally finding it very difficult and sometimes impossible to meet their recruiting goals), loss or reduction of social values and norms, and political extremism bring down some governments. Examples include Iran in 1979, France in the late 18th Century, China in the late 1940s, and Mexico and Russia in the early 20th Century.

Sometimes governments just *quit* for a variety of reasons, resulting in ethnic fragmentation, like in the case of the Soviet Union.

Perhaps you noted that America is currently suffering from two of the three aforementioned reasons why countries fall, i.e., we are at war and are experiencing symptoms that sometimes lead to revolution.

Right now, America is fighting a type of war—global asymmetric warfare—that has never been fought before by any nation. Our enemies wear no uniforms, abide by no rules, attack civilian targets, are in 90 countries including our own, and want every American dead and the country destroyed.

We are suffering from political extremism mostly on the left; a clear reduction of social values and norms; widespread disillusionment when it comes to the war, social issues, politics, and the economy; and even some strife (a huge homeless population, high bankruptcy rate, a massive illegal alien population consisting of between 16 and 20 million people, etc.).

What makes many Americans think America is invulnerable to collapse or destruction? Such a belief is spectacularly arrogant.

History applies to all countries. According to history, we are far more at risk than what most Americans believe.

Extremists in the media (the *Denver Post*'s Reggie Rivers, the *Rocky Mountain News*' Jason Salzman, the *New York Times*' Tom Friedman, Paul Krugman, and Maureen Dowd, Bill Moyers, Air America's Al Franken, Michael Moore, Barbra Streisand, Tim Robbins, Sean Penn, Susan Sarandon, Ed Asner, et al), politics (Howard Dean, Sen. Dianne Feinstein, Rep. Barbara Boxer, Sen. Ted Kennedy, Sen. John Kerry, Sen.

Robert Byrd, et al), and our collective societal commode (Ward Churchill, Louis Farrakhan, et al) are trying to dramatically change America as we know it. From their influential (upon many Americans suffering from muddy thinking) positions, such radicals fuel the flames of hate and discontent among those who are repulsed by the very idea of the United States Constitution and the Bill of Rights. Fury, frustration, and disbelief replace reason and respect when these types are forced to accept major political losses and when they realize most Americans disagree with their fanatical agendas. The left's shrill fanaticism acts as an accelerant in creating an emotional inferno among the followers of such would-be tyrants, which increases the chances of America falling while advancing the time line for our demise.

Nevertheless, many if not most Americans, in their complacency and ignorance of history, believe we have no reason to worry; that America will always exist regardless of history and the threats currently facing our nation.

How very, very wrong they are.

Some day America, too, will fall. This might happen centuries from now, decades from now, a few years from now or next week.

The trick is postponing the inevitable. What can America do to delay what will one day surely occur?

That is the question we should all be asking ourselves at this moment, but few are, which brings us right back to the aforementioned arrogance, complacency, and ignorance.

An arrogant, complacent, and ignorant people is its own worst enemy, a fact history and fate are counting on.

A 10-Point Plan to Win the War on Terror

This chapter will no doubt cause the radical left, which has no genuine interest whatsoever in winning the war on terror, to wig out. Anti-freedom extremist organizations like the American Civil Liberties Union, Human Rights Watch, Amnesty International, MoveOn.org, Democratic National Committee, et al will call for my head and accost me with pejorative monikers because I have the gall to coldly calculate what steps need to be taken to mercilessly crush the enemy and call for their implementation.

Points 1 through 9 are mandatory in that failure to accomplish any one of them will likely result in primary objective denial.

Point 10 is desirable but optional.

POINT 1
The Border, Port, and Coastal Security Act

The Border, Port, and Coastal Security Act is required to mandate, at the federal level, sufficient defensive assets (monetary, logistical, technical, and personnel) to thwart the vast majority of possible planned acts of terrorism or terrorist-act support efforts intending to exploit America's nearly defenseless land borders, ports, and coastlines.

POINT 2
The Immigration and Visa Reform Act

The Immigration and Visa Reform Act is required to dramatically reduce opportunities for terrorists to exploit our current immigration and visa policies that allow terrorists and those who secretly support terrorists to legally enter the United States on a visa or become resident aliens or naturalized citizens.

POINT 3
Terrorist-Haven Nation Accountability and Interdiction Policy

It must become the policy of the United States to aggressively and continually hold nations knowingly and willingly providing terrorists with a safe haven, fully accountable for their actions via military, economic, and diplomatic sanctions. Furthermore, the United States military must be used to interdict, regardless of their location, all terrorist groups and organizations and persons who support such groups.

POINT 4
Domestic Muslim Organizations Assessment Policy

With assistance from other U.S. law-enforcement, homeland security and intelligence agencies, the Federal Bureau of Investigation must use all its assets to conduct effective counterterrorism operations against Muslim organizations in the United States suspected of terrorist activities of any kind, to include moral support and encouragement of terrorists. Undercover infiltration and electronic intelligence gathering, as well as other forms of covert surveillance and monitoring, must be employed.

POINT 5
War-On-Terror Operational Capabilities Expansion

The U.S. military must substantially expand its ability to conduct counterterrorism operations in the realm of global asymmetric warfare. This should be accomplished by adding, at a minimum, one expeditionary brigade to the Marine Corps and fully activating the 4th Marine Division, and adding two brigades to the Army. Additionally, a major increase in special operations forces (Army Special Forces or "Green Berets," Army Rangers, Navy SEALs, and Marine Corps Force Recon units) and a major increase in the operational capabilities of the CIA's Special Activities Division must be aggressively undertaken.

POINT 6
Terrorist Head-of-State Termination Program

The president of the United States, with or without the support of the Congress, must immediately authorize and direct by any and all means necessary short of nuclear weapons employment, the removal from power of any head-of-state found to be supporting acts of terror against the United States and its allies. This policy must include selective target acquisition and termination.

POINT 7
Government Employee Accountability Act

The Government Employee Accountability Act must be enacted to expeditiously dismiss from government employment any and all employees, regardless of position and pay grade, for substandard performance. Any employee determined to be derelict, negligent, or incompetent in their duties will have their employment immediately terminated and an investigation will ensue to determine how that former employee came to be in that position. Any government employee found to be negligent in the hiring of a substandard employee will also be dismissed or reduced in grade.

POINT 8
Journalist and Media Accountability Policy

Any person within the U.S. media suspected of being in possession of classified government material will be immediately and fully investigated along with their parent media company. Media representatives, supervisors, and their parent companies found to be in possession of said material will be arrested and charged under the U.S. Code.

POINT 9
Critical Target Vulnerability Assessment Program

A program of vulnerability assessments on the nation's critical targets must be instituted. High-value, high-risk targets likely or known to be of interest to terrorists must be evaluated for their vulnerability and corrective defensive action taken, with special attention being paid to targets that would, if successfully attacked, cause substantial loss of life and/or economic damage on a national level.

POINT 10
Sea-Based Prisoners of War Program

All illegal-combatant prisoners of war held by the United States should be held totally incommunicado and with no third-party access whatsoever in prison ships always in international waters. This program would dramatically reduce intelligence leaks, aid the interrogation process, and reduce the "distraction" level produced by third-party interference.

* * *

Shocked?

Stunned that I would even contemplate such harsh, controversial actions?

Mortified that a Marine would figure out how to dramatically increase his nation's combat power at the strategic level and then have the nerve to actually publish it, knowing full well that his nation's enemies, both foreign and domestic, would go bananas upon reading it?

Aghast that a grunt-turned-media-type could somehow cut through the crap and not only determine where our major weaknesses are, but then lay out a plan of action that, if brought to bear, would stagger the enemy?

Why?

You shouldn't be.

Marines have been coming up with seemingly crazy schemes since 1775. Those schemes tend to work, in case you have never read Marine Corps history. We are trained to think outside of the proverbial box and to disregard controversy caused by the maniacal plots we hatch. We tend to ignore squawking, posturing politicians and the screaming, wild-eyed left of today. Dimwitted diplomats, Democrat dandies, and limp-wristed liberals must be made to understand that, to win this war on terror, we must abandon their kinder, gentler, politically correct, overly sensitive approach to dealing with our foes and go straight for the jugular with the sharpened edge of an extended entrenching tool swung by some Leatherneck goon named Lance Corporal Bruno Klutcher who was raised in an alley in the Bronx.

The bottom line is that if we, as a nation, follow this 10-point plan, far fewer Americans and far more terrorists will die in this melee called global asymmetric warfare.

Believe it.

Bibliography

Bossie, David N. *Intelligence Failure: How Clinton's National Security Policy Set the Stage for 9/11*. Nashville: WND, 2004. A good look at how Bill Clinton's policies and personal shortcomings led to 9-11.

Gertz, Bill: *Breakdown: How America's Intelligence Failures Led to September 11*. Washington, DC: Regnery, 2002. One of the best on what caused the worst terrorist attack in history.

Gertz, Bill. *Treachery: How America's Friends and Foes Are Secretly Arming Our Enemies*. New York: Crown Forum, 2004. An excellent examination of what our pals and enemies are up to by the well-known investigative reporter from the *Washington Times*.

Gunaratna, Rohan. *Inside Al Qaeda: Global Network of Terror*. London: Hurst, 2002. A very good insider's look by the world's leading authority on al Qaeda.

Hunt, David. *They Just Don't Get It: How Washington Is Still Compromising Your Safety—and What You Can Do About It*. New York: Crown Forum, 2005. Colonel Hunt's typically blunt assessment of how government bureaucracy, incompetence, and dereliction of duty continues to place America at extreme risk.

Koopman, John. *McCoy's Marines: Darkside to Baghdad*. St. Paul: Zenith, 2004. The best, most gripping account by an embedded reporter in Iraq. Koopman's book will make you scream, cry, and laugh like hell, as well as make you start to understand what life is like as a combat Marine.

Kushner, Harvey. *Holy War on the Home Front: The Secret Islamic Terror Network in the United States*. New York: Sentinel, 2004. An infuriating look at little-known facts about al Qaeda remaining here in the homeland, even after 9-11.

Malkin, Michelle. *Invasion: How America Still Welcomes Terrorists, Criminals, and Other Foreign Menaces to Our Shores*. Washington, DC: Regnery, 2002. The best book available on just how out-of-control or border security and immigration situation is, despite all the warnings.

McInerney, Thomas and Paul Vallely. *Endgame: The Blueprint for Victory in the War on Terror*. Washington, DC: Regnery, 2004. This is a solid book on how the war on terror could be won, written by two retired generals and current FOX News Channel analysts.

Miniter, Richard. *Losing Bin Laden: How Bill Clinton's Failures Unleashed Global Terror*. Washington, DC: Regnery, 2003. Read this and you are going to want to kick Bill Clinton right in the shins.

Miniter, Richard. *Shadow War: The Untold Story of How Bush Is Winning the War on Terror*. Washington, DC: Regnery, 2004. Miniter's superb and insightful report on matters pertaining to the war on terror that the left-wing media would rather you didn't know.

Newman, Bob. *Guerrillas in the Mist: A Battlefield Guide to Clandestine Warfare*. Boulder: Paladin, 1997. A guerrilla warfare manual written from the guerrilla's perspective. Lots of history and practical information.

Newman, Bob. *Trenches and Hard-Points*. Frederick, MD: PublishAmerica, 2002. A Gulf War novel based on true events.

About the Author

One of the world's most respected authorities on terrorism, guerrilla warfare, special operations, survival, and security, Bob Newman has been commended for his work by mayors, governors, senators, congressional representatives, and generals, including Gen. Richard B. Myers, the former chairman of the Joint Chiefs of Staff. He has given briefings and presentations on terrorism at the prestigious Intelligence Summit, Maritime Security Council's International Maritime Security Summit, China Shipping 2004, Intersec Security Exposition, Airport-Port-Terminal Security (Middle East) Exposition & Conference, TOC-Asia (Terminal Operations Conference—Asia), U.S. Air Force Academy, and to various business organizations as well as an assortment of government (foreign and domestic), media, civic, and private entities. A terrorism, weapons of mass destruction, and tactics consultant to one of the largest metropolitan police departments in the United States, he is also the Director of International Security & Counterterrorism Services for The GeoScope Group, which provides Vulnerability Assessment Teams from the world's most elite law enforcement agencies, intelligence organizations, and military special operations units.

The host of Denver's top-rated evening news-talk program (the "Gunny Bob Show" on Newsradio 850 KOA) and an award-winning military science and terrorism analyst,

Bob's hard-hitting, insightful analysis and commentary on terrorism, homeland security, guerrilla warfare, and military science has resulted in his appearances on such programs as "The O'Reilly Factor," "On the Record" with Greta van Susteren, "War Zone" with Geraldo Rivera, "FOX News Live," "FOX News Sunday" and "Big Story Weekend" with Rita Cosby, "War on Terror: The Hunt for the Killers" with Linda Vester and Laurie Dhue, "The Big Story" with John Gibson, "The FOX Report" with Shepard Smith, ABC's "World News Tonight," MSNBC's "Connected Coast to Coast" (hosted by Ron Reagan Jr. and Monica Crowley), CNN, the "Today" show (interviewed by Matt Lauer), "Talkback Live," "Catherine Crier Live," "Montel Williams," "Cochran & Company," and radio stations from coast to coast as well as in Europe and Australia.

In October of 2002, Bob was the counterterrorism consultant for an investigative report on terrorism and homeland security for CBS in Phoenix. In July of 2003, *Newsweek*'s World Wide Web edition published an extensive interview with him on asymmetric warfare in Iraq. Bob is a popular political columnist for Frontiers of Freedom and Men's News Daily. The *Chicago Tribune* repeatedly consulted Bob in 2004 about interrogation techniques, the Geneva Conventions, and myriad aspects of subjects relating to Abu Ghraib and Guantanamo Bay. While in the Middle East in March 2005, he was extensively interviewed by Reuters and Agence France-Presse regarding terrorism in the Persian Gulf.

Bob is well known for his uncanny ability to precisely predict the nature and location (by country) of terrorist attacks months, even years in advance, as well as antiterrorist operations carried out by the U.S. Department of Defense (DoD) and/or Central Intelligence Agency and events relating to standard DoD operations, such as Operation Iraqi Freedom. He is also the most successful investigative journalist covering the war on terror, with 100+ accurate predictions and assessments as well as stories he has broken since October 2001 (more than all other military science and terrorism analysts in the media).

Bob won a national-level 2002 Edward R. Murrow Award for investigative reporting on terrorism and homeland security and a 2001 Associated Press/Colorado Broadcasters Association Award, also for investigative reporting on terrorism and homeland security. In 2003, "Redmond & Newman" won a Colorado Broadcasters Association Award of Excellence. In 2004, Bob won another Colorado Broadcasters Association Award of Excellence for his special live broadcast on the first anniversary of the beginning of the liberation of Iraq titled "365 Days of War." In 2005, Bob won a third Colorado Broadcasters Assocation Award of Excellence, this time in the Best Evening Show category in a metro market. He has been consulted by the BBC on terrorism, interrogations, and guerrilla warfare; was selected by *Westword* as the "Best Military Expert" in that publication's 2002 "Best of Denver" competition; and is a recipient of the Sergeant Major of the Marine Corps' Leadership Writing Award.

The author of nearly 2,000 articles and columns that have appeared in dozens of publications, as well as 19 nonfiction books, including the popular *Guerrillas in the Mist: A Battlefield Guide to Clandestine Warfare, Marine Special Warfare and Elite Unit Tactics,* and *Wilderness Wayfinding: How to Survive in the Wilderness as You Travel,* his first novel, *Trenches and Hard-Points* (a Gulf War novel), was released in October 2002. A correspondent for the Cybercast News Service, Bob's investigative reports on everything from terrorism to medicine are known for their depth and insight.

In March 2005, Bob accepted the position of adjunct scholar at The Institute for Liberty, a conservative think tank. Bob is also a popular guest instructor at Metropolitan State College in Denver, where he lectures on political science, history, culture, Islam, Judaism, and terrorism.

Bob has briefed members of Congress and their staffs on homeland security and the war on terror as they pertain to immigration reform. His "10-Point Plan to Win the War on Terror" has raised eyebrows on Capitol Hill and has been noted by the Congressional Immigration Reform Caucus.

Dave Kopel of the *Rocky Mountain News*, who is also an associate policy analyst for the Cato Institute and a columnist for *National Review Online*, said: "In the Colorado media, KOA evening radio host Bob Newman is virtually alone in presenting a sophisticated understanding of military science."

A certified hostage survival instructor, Bob is a decorated, retired parachute- and scuba-qualified United States Marine with extensive, global operational experience in reconnaissance, special operations, counterterrorism, and wilderness survival, and is a ground combat veteran who has traveled to 43 countries.

He makes his home in Colorado with his wife, Susan, and daughter, Britta.